Thr̲e̲e̲

Marches
Way

Les Lumsdon

Published by Sigma Leisure – an imprint of
Sigma Press, 1 South Oak Lane, Wilmslow, Cheshire SK9 6AR, England.

Whilst every effort has been made to ensure that the information given in this book is correct, neither the publisher nor the author accept any responsibility for any inaccuracy.

British Library Cataloguing in Publication Data
A CIP record for this book is available from the British Library.

ISBN: 1-85058-269-6

Typesetting and Design by: Sigma Press, Wilmslow, Cheshire.

Maps by: Pam Upchurch

Photographs: by the author, except where indicated.

Cover design: Martin Mills

Printed by:
Manchester Free Press, Paragon Mill, Jersey St., Manchester M4 6FP.

CONTENTS

Acknowledgements:

The author wishes to thank the following organisations for their assistance in the preparation of Marches Way:

Cheshire County Council (special thanks to Helen Crowe and Mike Nutkins), North Shropshire District Council
Shropshire County Council (special thanks to Terry Hughes, John Newnham, Peter Clark, Jacky Brooks and Lesley Davies)
Hereford and Worcester County Council (special thanks to Geoff Allen and Mike Radford)
Gwent County Council (special thanks to Kim Colebrook, Mike Longridge and Chris Barber)
Mid Glamorgan (special thanks to Dai Workman)
The Forestry Commission and The National Trust
The Countryside Council for Wales
The Wales Tourist Board and several Rambling groups.

Thanks also go to numerous organisations who took time out to respond to my enquiries and supply photographs.

THE MARCHES

A journey through The Marches reveals a subtle charm hard to find elsewhere. For this is a landscape worked by local farming families throughout the ages, disturbed only by the warring of the powerful Norman Marcher Lords and the upheavals brought by the English Civil War.

For the most part, life has gone on at a tranquil pace, little changed throughout the centuries. Villages remain sleepy and the countryside as peaceful as ever. Admittedly, during the past decades there have been more dramatic changes. Traffic, for example, has increased. In the borderlands, it is confined to a handful of major routes and in the congested cities. The back lanes of the countryside, often festooned with clover, plantain, vetches and rose hips, are as quiet now as they were in earlier times.

Farming is the main occupation of The Marches. In recent decades it has become mechanised and, as a result, there are far fewer workers on the land. However, despite mechanisation, many of the early field patterns have been retained, some of which date back to medieval times or earlier. The weather-beaten hillsides are still dominated by sheep farming, with world famous breeds such as Clun and Ryeland - but in the richer lowland areas, mixed cropping has become more prevalent, but cattle rearing is still important. Thankfully, home orchards, riverside pastures and woodland break up the landscape and make walking such a joy throughout the route.

Where is The Marches?

The word almost certainly derives from the Anglo Saxon "Mearc" denoting a boundary and became more commonly used some years after the Norman conquest of England. The Marches stretches from the borders of Cheshire to the Severn estuary as depicted by the map on page 12. It is part of seven predominantly rural counties – Cheshire, Clwyd, Shropshire, Powys, Hereford and Worcester, Gloucestershire and

Gwent. As a destination area, it is referred to in the 'singular', in the text, i.e. a collection of borderland counties known as one tourist location.

Current tourism brochures tend to describe it as an undiscovered place. This is not strictly correct, the area has always had appeal to the visitor. Victorian travel writers came here too. They came with the railways to explore these wilder parts of western England and Mid-Wales. They spent, perhaps, less time in The Marches than in Snowdonia or Lakeland where the heavenly climbs and sparkling lakes brought instant reward. Nevertheless, early gazetteers suggest that visits to spa towns such as Church Stretton and Llandrindod Wells or to popular beauty spots on the Wye or Severn were in vogue. Witness the extract from one of the Murray Travel Companion handbooks refering to Church Stretton in the 1870s:

"(The area) ... can be considered an epitome of England, for it contains within the compass of a few miles all the characteristics of an Alpine district in miniature, while at the same time orchards, gardens and farmhouses."

This is the appeal of The Marches. The landscape is so varied. The Welsh mountains give way to gently unfolding foothills, truncated by bubbling infant rivers, the Onny, Arrow, Monnow and Ebbw, soon meandering to the outwash lowlands plains.

The impetus to open up this truly rural area of England and Wales to visitors has been championed again in more recent times. Tourism authorities during the past ten years have developed a visitor campaign branded as "The Marches . . . Where England and Wales Meet". It sounds more romantic than the Welsh Borderlands. But this is not a place for mass tourism and most people concerned accept it. The Marches is very unspoilt. Its small rural towns still function as meeting places for the agricultural community. There are all manner of livestock and poultry markets and general street stalls to be found in the Marcher towns.

Places such as Abergavenny, Leominster and Wem still have dozens of small independently owned shops in their main thoroughfares, offering a wide variety of goods. It is a wonder that they have resisted the onslaught of modern development and the domination of major retail chains which seem to be omnipresent in almost every High street. But they have. The towns of The Marches have managed to retain their identity and character. Even those with more of a tourist heritage such as Church Stretton or Ludlow have not succumbed entirely to the marketplace but have maintained that delicate balance between the needs of resident and visitor without alienating either group.

The major cities and towns have had their effect. Shrewsbury and Hereford have an unbelievable number of supermarkets, many now sited by intrusive new roads on their outskirts. These sites are designed to draw people from miles around. Despite this, the village shop has survived in many places. It is the villages of the Marches that make this long distance walk so fascinating. They are a storehouse of historic interest and usually have a place of refreshment and accommodation to suit limited numbers of visitors. Villages such as Schocklach, Pulverbatch, Yarpole, Ewyas Harold and Llanover all have different tales to tell and the walker should stay awhile to absorb the atmosphere. Those who like the idea of a "Country Village Weekend Break" might care to pick up a leaflet at one of the tourist information centres in The Marches. This excellent idea of staying with villagers for a weekend, enjoying their company, local walks, culture and crafts was dreamed up by Eardisley resident David Gorvett in the early 1980s to stimulate interest and wealth in local village economies. May the scheme flourish.

Changing Times

Historians would argue that the decline of rural communities began in the last century but that the real impact has occured during the past thirty years. Gone are many wayside inns and post office cum stores, community schools and agricultural workshops. Gone too are the thrice daily village bus and small town cinema. The loss of such facilities has been compounded by a steady decline of population and, in particular, of younger people moving away for jobs. The drift has not been stemmed. There has also been an influx of early retirers and thus bringing a considerable change in the balance of the age profile.

Recent small scale housing and industrial developments in larger villages have helped to stabilise matters, as has the growth of rural tourism. Such limited development could well stimulate a mixed economy of agriculture, related light industry and tourism. It might encourage people to stay rather than commute long distances each day to seek work.

Acton Scott Historic Working Farm

What has been miraculously preserved in many villages is the distinct vernacular architecture of the borderlands and, in particular, half-timbered housing as well as Georgian and Victorian red brick buildings of character. Settlements nestled around parish churches, often built on sites dating back to the earliest of times, are common on the route.

Walking between these villages adds to the dimension of the route for the personality of each community differs.

Marcher Lords

The Marches has not always been peaceful. It has witnessed turbulent times. The Romans came to establish frontier communities such as Isca at Caerleon, Magnis at Kenchester (near Hereford) and Deva (Chester) to police tribes and hold down warrior leaders such as Caracticus. Offa's Dyke, is another reminder of the borderland struggles, built by the King of Mercia in the eight century as a boundary to contain the Welsh to mountainous regions rather then the lusher lowlands of Shropshire and Herefordshire. Offa was no more successful, however, than the Normans who came in the 12th century to calm both the English and Welsh. William the Conqueror established the powerful Marcher lords who ruled from magnificent castles. These were built strategically throughout the borders, sometimes reinforcing earlier sites used by the English.

These Marcher lords not only fought the Welsh in skirmish after skirmish but also fought between themselves to gain ascendancy and power with or against the monarch of the age. The number of motte and bailey castles, some with surviving stonework, some simply tree clad mounds, bear witness to the degree of control exerted to finally bring stability to the area. A stability that lasted for centuries and even survived the internecine strife of the English Civil War.

Industrialisation came to The Marches but only in small pockets, and on a small scale. The cities of Hereford and Shrewsbury enjoyed growth through manufacturing as did Newport as a port. Most other towns in The Marches continued much as before with only incremental growth. The rail network superseded the canals, but many of the railway branches simply remained as lines to nowhere which closed earlier in many instances than the Beeching era. Motorways have not penetrated the area to any great extent for there is no economic justification although the lobbying to upgrade roads continues regardless.

Thus, The Marches has remained quiet and this is its beauty. And what better way to see it than on foot!

The Walk

The 204 mile route begins at Chester and finishes at Cardiff. It is designed not only for the walker seeking a long distance route for holiday purposes but for also very much for weekend and day walking. Thus, it threads between stations on The Marches railway line so that walks of this nature can be planned with ease, using the train to allow point to point rambling. There are opportunities for short walks between stations and cut-off points are mentioned throughout the text. These are summarised below:

SHORT WALKS:

CHESHIRE

	Kms	Transport
Chester to Eccleston	7	Local bus from Chester
Eccleston to Farndon	10	Local buses from Chester
Farndon to Malpas	13	Local buses from Chester
Malpas to Whitchurch	12	Local bus

SHROPSHIRE

	Kms	Transport
Whitchurch to Prees	9	Local train
Prees to Wem	10	Local train
Wem to Yorton	9	Local train
Yorton to Bomere Heath	10	Local train/bus to & from Shrewsbury
Bomere to Shrewsbury	9	Local bus
Shrewsbury to Pontesbury	15	Local bus
Pontesbury to Church Stretton	19	Local bus/train to/from Shrewsbury
Church Stretton to Craven Arms	16	Local train
Craven Arms to Onibury	10	Local Bus
Onibury to Ludlow	10	Local Bus
Ludlow to Luston	19	Local Bus
Luston to Leominster	8	Local Bus
Leominster to Dinmore	15	Local Bus
Dinmore to Hereford	18	Local Bus
Hereford to Kingstone	10	Local Bus

Kingstone to Ewyas Harold	10	Local Buses to/from Hereford
Ewyas Harold to Pandy	10	Local Buses to/from Hereford
Pandy to Abergavenny	14	Local Bus
Abergavenny to Llanover	12	Local Bus
Llanover to Pontypool	14	Local Bus
Pontypool to Caerleon	15	Local Bus to Newport
Newport to Draethen	13	Local Bus to Little Machen
Draethen to Tongwynlais	13	Local Bus to Little Machen/Train to Cardiff
Tongwynlais to Cardiff	10	Local Bus from Cardiff/ Valley Lines Train to Radyr

WHAT TO EXPECT

Marches Way is an unofficial long distance path. It was first sketched out as a possible route in 1989, researched in 1990, and a final route decided upon in 1991 and re-walked accordingly. Throughout the route the respective County Councils responsible for rights of ways have been informed and have taken on the necessary clearance work to make the route viable. This will be an ongoing exercise.

In Cheshire, the County Council decided to waymark the route for which the author is most grateful and the Marches Way waymark is likely to be seen in countryside locations between Chester and Grindley Brook. The other County Councils have chosen not to do this but to use standard waymarking where remedial work has been undertaken on paths. Thus, in places the route will be clearly marked and in good order. In other places, the walker will not be given this level of guidance in terms of signposting nor waymarking. The use of barred gates is common along certain sections and at times the walker will find that the route uses gaps in hedges where stiles once stood or where bits of fencing now act as stiles.

This should not deter from the enjoyment. It is slower opening barred gates or negotiating awkward stiles but the right of way should be clear. The route has been checked against the definitive maps held at each county council. Therefore, the walker will find variations in a few places when reading the Pathfinder maps.

The major issue which often irritates the reader is when things change on the ground. Since researching the route County authorities have agreed to improve sections and therefore a stile might be present where a gateway worked before, for example.

Marches Way also traverses working farmland. This brings changes. Pools might be filled in, field hedges grubbed and derelict cottages and barns re-built thus rendering the description in the book slightly inaccurate. Regardless, the description should be sufficiently detailed to cope with such changes. The rotation of crops can be a problem if it brings obstruction to a path. It is no fun walking through a wet field of cereal and is virtually impossible to negotiate rape oil seed at any time. The farmer should by law reinstate a path across a field in arable crop and you are entitled to walk in the line of the path delineated by the definitive footpath map. Please report such obstructions so that others do not have to encounter this. The author intends to walk vulnerable sections and do just this to ensure that the route is acceptable.

Many of the paths chosen are lightly walked at present and a very small minority of farmers can take exception to increased levels of walking on their land. The result can be obstructions such as little bits of barbed wire. Once again, you are entitled to walk around the obstruction to gain access to the next section of the route. Marches Way goes through very few farms but where passing a farm yard or country cottage please pass with consideration.

One final point. Perception is an uncanny thing. The author might well describe a section of route without recourse to one landmark which is important to you, the reader, and therefore could lead to a misunderstanding in terms of direction. If you do find yourself going astray retrace your steps to the point where the route felt right to you and re read the instructions seeking another way. Curse the author momentarily and proceed on the route!

Country Pubs

Most country pubs on or near the pub are included in the guide. In the main, they welcome walkers and offer a tasty selection of fine beers and other beverages, in addition to a variety of food. This is based on exhaustive research by the author! Where opening times and other details are shown it means that the publican(s) has been kind enough to return a questionnaire in a pre-paid envelope supplied to the author. These people obviously take care to get things right. Others are included but they have not returned any information. This does not mean that they will not welcome the walker! Town pubs have not been included but there are dozens of lovely pubs in the Marcher towns so do not be timid in your exploration.

Traditional Brews

Those of you who walk to enjoy a good pint will not be disappointed on Marches Way. There are several local independent brewers in The Marches. In Hereford, for example, the Wye Valley Brewery and the Jolly Roger Brewery stand within throwing distance of each other. Brains in Cardiff offer good ales throughout South Wales and the town of Wem offers Hanby ales in free houses in North Shropshire.

The attitude of many of these breweries is summed up by Edward Wood, of Wood Brewery at Wistanstow, Craven Arms (the brewery tap, The Plough, is a mile off the route):

"Brewing here involves the use of only the finest ingredients and traditional methods. The 100 percent malt grist is produced with prime barley and extracted with local water in a mash tun. We also use Herefordshire hops. It is the care taken at every stage that makes a flavoursome beer."

Long live the tradition!

There are a few things that all publicans comment about. They are in business and depend heavily on food trade to make a living. Thus, they do not like people eating their own food on the premises. Ramblers, for some unknown reason, seem to have a bad reputation for this. Food is served in most establishments at lunchtime and in the evening but not for the full session, i.e. food tends to be served between noon and 2 pm at lunch and not after 9 – 9.30 pm in the evenings.

Almost all have outdoor drinking areas suitable for families and most welcome well behaved children. They do not necessarily have a place indoors set aside for families, i.e. separate from a bar as dictated by law. So please do not be offended, it is the law. If you are walking as a family its worthwhile just popping a head around the door to check first. Finally, dirty boots and large rucksacks need to be left outside or in the porch.

The author was particularly impressed by the number of lovely gardens and outside drinking areas offered by inns and pubs throughout The Marches. With the recent warm summers, it is a joy to sit and relax far away from the madding crowd at a country pub.

ACCOMMODATION

Accommodation is available on or near to the route for almost the entire length. Places, rather than establishments, offering accommodation are noted in each chapter. But it is best to contact the relevant Tourist Information Centre for an up-to-date list of accommodation in the area as there is bound to be more farmhouse bed and breakfast than mentioned in this guide. Listed below are the key Tourist Information Centres:

Chester: Town Hall, Northgate Street. Tel: (0244) 318356.

Whitchurch: The Civic Centre. Tel: (0948) 4577.

Shrewsbury: The Music Hall. Tel: (0743) 350761.

Church Stretton: Church Street. Tel: (0694) 723133.*

Ludlow: Castle Street. Tel: (0584) 875053.

Leominster: School Lane. Tel: (0568) 616460.

Hereford: St Owens Street. Tel: (0432) 268430.

Abergavenny: Swan Meadow. Tel: (0873) 857588.*

Newport: John Frost Square. Tel: (0633) 842962.

Cardiff: Bridge Street. Tel: (0222) 227281.

* Seasonal Opening only.

BRITISH RAILWAYS

Enquiries:

Chester (0244) 340170
Shrewsbury (0743) 364041
Newport (0633) 842222
Cardiff (0222) 228000

Planning The Route

The planning of the route is part of the fun so the author has resisted the temptation of setting rigid frameworks to follow. The beauty of the route is that local trains and buses are available for the best part of the route for those seeking overnight stops in the main towns. For example, the walker might decide to finish walking at Yorton and then travel into Shrewsbury for the evening.

Hardened walkers could walk the route in a week. Those wishing to saunter and take a break here and there will find that 10 to 14 days is preferable. Achieving ten to fifteen miles a day is ideal for most people and not all of the route has to be walked in one attempt. Enjoy your walk!

Long Distance Paths

Marches Way joins or crosses the following long distance paths:

Sandstone Trail – At Tushingham
Shropshire Way – At Whitchurch and several places in Shropshire
Black and White Trail – At Leominster
Wye Valley Walk – At Hereford
Offa's Dyke Trail – At Llanfihangel
Usk Valley Walk – At Llanfoist
Sirhowy Valley Walk – At Rogerstone
Rhymney Valley Ridgeway Walk – At Draethen
Cambrian Way – Tongwynlais
Taff Valley Heritage Trail – Tongwynlais

Location Map

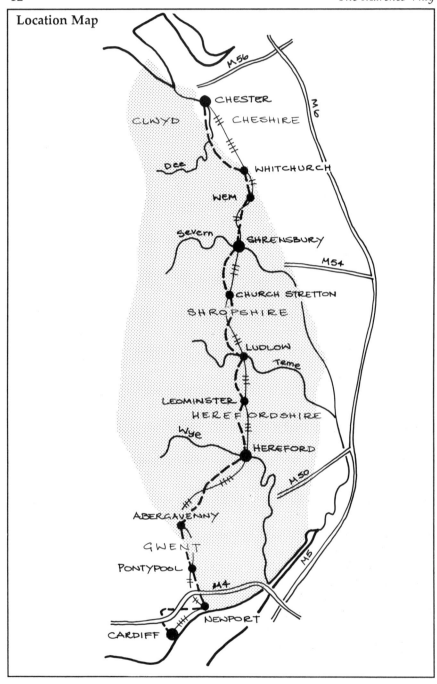

CHESTER TO FARNDON

START: Chester Railway Station

DISTANCE: 17 km (11 mls)

MAPS: Pathfinder Maps 774 Chester (East), and 790 Farndon, Holt and Tattenhall

ROUTE DESCRIPTION

A walk through Chester, along the Shropshire Union Canal, and beneath the city walls, hence avoiding the traffic. Across the Dee and then following a riverside path known to the Victorians to Eccleston and the Iron Bridge, an ornate bridge on the Eaton Estate. The walk continues along paths and back lanes to the outskirts of Farndon where it crosses market garden fields to the village.

FEATURES

Chester

Chester enjoys its heritage. Despite local government reform in the 1970s it still manages to elect a mayor who also happens to be Admiral of the Dee, known more for its pleasure boats than its trading vessels these days. The city is very appealing and hence becomes very busy (that's being polite) with visitors in summer and with shoppers before Christmas. It is not surprising as the city is steeped in antiquity and has preserved so many different monuments and buildings from Roman excavations to fine Georgian houses.

Chester is a fun place to visit if you don't mind the crowds. Try one of the excellent guided town walks to whet the appetite, then visit one of the many museums and attractions or simply spend an afternoon lolling by the river. The remainder of Marches Way is exceedingly quiet by comparison.

Eccleston

The Roman Road, Watling Street, passed through this settlement, which is now very much an estate village marking a boundary of Eaton Hall.

The village post office was once a public house, but the first Duke of Westminster is said to have closed it to stop excessive drinking in the neighbourhood. The church standing today was rebuilt at the behest of the very same Duke in the year of his death, 1899. He is said to have requested "a small cathedral". The wrought iron entrance gates are nothing short of magnificent, having originally been built in the eighteenth century for Emral Hall in Clwyd and re-located as a memorial to the second duke who died in 1953. An early jester to the family is said to have lodged himself on a branch in the village (as jesters do) and then chopped it off (the branch) in the front of the crowd. Needless to say, he died as a result and his epitaph reads:

> Poor Jack lies beneath this rood and sure he must be blessed,
> For if he could do nothing good he meant to do his best,
> Think of your souls ye guilty throng who,
> Knowing what is right, do wrong.

Eaton Hall

The modern building of the 1970s, succeeding several previous halls, blends very well with earlier structures belonging to the Grosvenor family. Fortunately, the splendid landscaped gardens are open to the public on selected sundays during the year. Earlier Dukes of Westminster were well known for their love of race horses and patronage of racecourses (the walk passes Eaton Stud farm) including The Roodee in Chester. The Iron Bridge, on the route, is typical of the many works added to this landscape during the past two hundred years. Just beyond is the estate village of Alford with its fine Victorian church standing near a motte surviving from earlier times when military presence counted.

Churton

The small village is characterised by half timbered houses. It is said to have grown substantially with an influx of workers to build and service Eaton estate. It hasn't a parish church but the walk passes by a Methodist chapel.

Farndon

Also on the Roman road, English Farndon stands opposite Welsh Holt on the banks of the Dee. The large village or small town has an unusual set of shops from a music centre to a clock repairer. The village was once home to John Speed, a sixteenth century cartographer and writer. Another local hero was Major Barnston who, according to local despatches of the time, fought valiantly in The Crimean War and then succumbed in the Indian Mutiny. The monument seen on the approach to the village is dedicated to him. The area still specialises in market garden crops and at one time was a major strawberry growing centre. Lovers of brass will know that the Farndon Brass Band has for some years been very popular.

REFRESHMENT:

Chester has all manner of food and drink places, Eccleston has none and at the time of writing Alford's pub had just closed. The **White Horse** at Churton is open Mondays to Saturdays from 11.30 am (Sundays from noon) until 3 pm and then from 5.30 pm in the evenings (Sundays 7 pm). Food is generally served every day and draught Bass is available.

There are three hostelries in Farndon almost within a stone's throw of each other. Between them, they offer a comprehensive range of facilities for the walker.

The Raven – This historic hotel, well known to local ramblers and cyclists is usually open from 11.00 am until 3.30 pm and from 5.30 pm on Monday to Fridays and all day on Saturdays. Usual hours on Sundays. Serves James Foreshaw and Stones bitter on draught and food. At one hour's notice, a special picnic can be prepared including a half bottle of wine. Accommodation is available, (0829) 270570. Gents beware. A ghost frequents the men's toilet, even though it is said to have been exorcised in earlier times!

The Nags Head – Open 11.30 until 3 pm on Mondays to Saturdays, and from 5.30 pm on Monday-Friday (7pm on Saturdays). Usual hours on Sundays. Pedigree bitter is available and food is served in this old brewery, now a cheery haunt for locals and visitors alike.

Greyhound Hotel – This CAMRA recommended hotel sells the Greenall Whitley range of beers on handpull and offers accommodation, (0829) 270244. It is open on weekend lunchtimes from noon until 3 pm but all evenings from 5.30 pm except Sunday, which is 7 pm. The hotel has several pets including two donkeys, Henry and Guinness who enjoy knocking back the waste beer! There are no facilities for children except those staying in the accommodation. Breakfasts are served for residents otherwise no food is available.

ACCOMMODATION – see above.

PUBLIC TRANSPORT

There is a regular bus service (but not Sundays) to Chester from Farndon (Nags Head) via Churton and Alford and also about five a day between Chester and Eccleston. Contact Cheshire Busline on (0244) 602666.

THE WALK

1.The walk starts from Chester railway station. From the station entrance walk ahead, across the mini roundabout and along City Road, where there are several hotels and guest houses. Walk on the left hand pavement to the bridge over the Shropshire Union canal, where the restored Steam Mill stands to your left. At the far end of the bridge drop down steps on the left to the towpath by an old fashioned pub, The Harkers Arms, and then bear left under the bridge.

2. The canal is something of a pedestrian thoroughfare in the mornings, as people stride out to work and school along the banks where boats have been moored for the night. At other times it is a tranquil corner away from the traffic. Pass a pub and Showboat restaurant where the canal curves right beneath King Charles Tower. It is said that the dear monarch of the same name watched his army being routed by the Parliamentarians at Rowton Moor from this vantage point. The canal flows into a deep cutting where two bridges can be seen overhead, one carrying Northgate Street and a smaller "Bridge of Sighs", which linked a chapel and a gaol. The one pity about this section is the occasional litter and dog fouling. Otherwise this is a splendid introduction to Chester.

3. As you approach the next less attractive concrete bridge, carrying part of the ring road, cut left up a path cobbled with setts and proceed under an arch in the ancient defensive walls. Cross the small access road to walk down the narrow Pemberton road to exit at King's Buildings. Turn

left here up the equally impressive King Street to emerge between two very old inns, The Red Lion and Pied Bull in Northgate.

4. Bear right and continue ahead along Northgate, with Chester Bus station to the right (for those who wish to bus it out of town), the Town Hall and Tourist Information Centre. This narrows to a pedestrianised section and into Eastgate, where the walker turns right by the old cross, and then first left into Bridge Street.

5. Go straight ahead at the next junction with Pepper Street into Lower Bridge Street and follow this to Bridgegate and the old Dee Bridge over the River Dee. Keep left and notice the weir, said to date originally from the eleventh century to control water for milling on the southern bank.

6. Opposite Bridge Cottages go left down steps to join a path along the riverside passing beneath modern apartments at first, then onwards towards an iron suspension bridge, built in the last century to link the city to Queens Park on the right. Across the river is an embankment known as The Groves, where boats take off for afternoon cruises and people sit sipping their drinks while watching the world go by. Keep ahead along the river, to walk by the riverside in open ground known as The Meadows (previously known as The Earl's Eye), fortunately bequeathed to the city by Mr and Mrs Brown in 1929 on the condition that it will always be used for recreation.

7. Simply follow the well worn riverside path as it leaves the city and through several fields before passing by a water extraction plant and then near to a 19th century house, known as Heronbridge. Keep to the river and after more fields pass beneath the portals of a modern road and Eccleston church can now be seen. The path continues ahead but those seeking a diversion into Eccleston should continue until a point past the church where a well worn and fenced path leads to the right into the village. Otherwise keep going!

8. Pass by the site of the old ferry, a turning point for many boaters and popular for the past hundred years when "Jimmy The Boat" ran a ferry crossing. Continue onwards to walk by Eaton stud farm, before following a track as it curves right through a wood, thus avoiding a lowland flood plain known as the Crook of Dee. To the right can be glimpsed the church tower of Eaton church which stands alongside Eaton Hall.

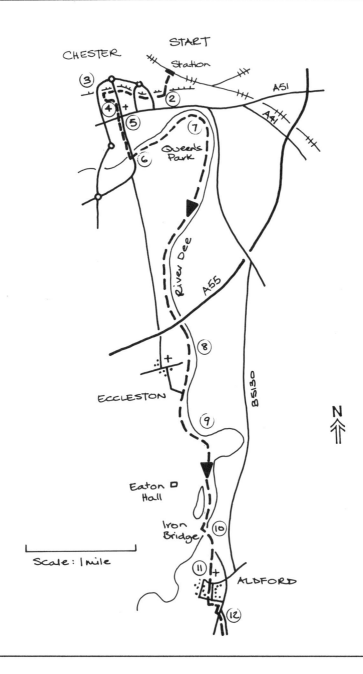

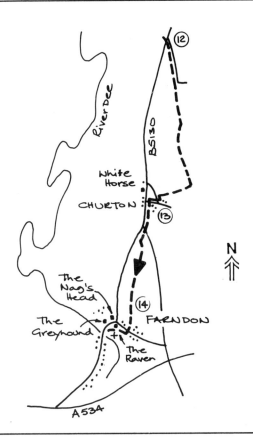

9. The track passes by a cottage on the right with the sweet scent of roses in the air. Walk ahead to a gate. This leads to a short woodland section and then the path moves closer to the banks of the pretty Dee again. This section can become lush in growth (including nettles), before the path curves to a track which leads left to join a road in a very short distance.

10. Go left here to cross the Iron Bridge, with a view of the lodge by the river and also over fields to the lofty Alford church ahead, a little to the right. Continue along the road, taking the right fork at the junction and at the end of the ghastly spread of rhododendrons, where the verge opens out, bear right to enter a field by a gate and then head slightly left, climbing very gently to the left of the earthworks, an early motte castle. Proceed through a kissing gate of sorts and then head towards the

church, bearing slightly right between the tree trunks, then aiming for the white gate to the right of the church.

11. Bear left onto the road and walk the few paces to a junction in the village. Turn left and walk past the post office and stores. Turn right to walk along a back lane and then left to walk down to the B5130 road passing by gardens tended with loving care and skill. Turn right and at the next junction turn left.

12. Follow this lane for a short distance before reaching another junction by a farm converted into offices. Go straight on along a track, known as Lower Lane, which soon becomes a green lane but eventually exits once again onto a metalled road. Go right here and right through a gate into a field. Cut directly across to a footbridge and cross it. The path leads up between a fence and a hedge and soon brings the walker to a lane. Turn left on it and follow this to a road by cottages in the village of Churton. Go left and then next right by a half timbered farmhouse. At the main road, the pub can be found to the right but unless stopping your way is to the left.

13. Walk along the pavement out of the village and pass by a junction. As the road curves more to the right go over the road to cross a stile leading into a field. Head slightly right to a stile in the next boundary. Then, walk ahead across a field, keeping parallel with a hedgerow on the left, which is soon joined by a tractor track. Go through a gap in the next boundary and keep ahead again across a large field, often cropped with market garden produce, heading towards a truncated hedge mid-field. Walk to the right of this hedge, still keeping ahead to cross a stile into a smaller field. Go straight on to cross another stile and then keep company with the hedge on the right as the path leads to a stile by houses.

14. Cross the stile and walk along a path between gardens and by an old converted mill down to a road. Cross the main road and walk down a road opposite, leading towards Farndon church and then ahead along a narrow lane down to the bridge. Those seeking refreshment should turn right by the church to walk the short distance into High Street.

FARNDON TO MALPAS

START: The Raven, High Street, Farndon

DISTANCE: 13 km (8 mls)

MAPS: Pathfinder Sheets 790 Farndon, Holt and Tattenhall, 807 Whitchurch and Malpas

ROUTE DESCRIPTION

The route hugs the Dee at first but then rises above the floodplain to follow a series of very old paths in Caldecott and Shocklach parishes. Marches Way continues through parkland, along bridle path to Overton Heath and a back lane and path to Malpas through delightful dairying country.

FEATURES

Shocklach

The very isolated church of Saint Edith is said to have been built by Thomas de Schocklach in the mid-twelfth century and certainly the exceptional south doorway belongs to this time. The church is associated with a 17th century recluse and theologian, John Dod, who prepared a commentary on the Decalogue in 1606. Throughout the centuries the place has been a sanctuary for forlorn travellers on foot. By the East window there is a message of thanks etched by two grateful eighteenth century wanderers who took refuge as the roads were so poor – "We were in danger of our lives". What pity that today the church is secured against vandals but a key can be obtained from the wardens. Still, it is not a place to be at still of night, for according to local legend a mysterious coach and horses is to be seen at the top of Church Road when a death is to happen in the village, almost a mile away. The centre of the population is thought to have moved away from the church at a time of severe plague. The cross in the churchyard could well have been a plague cross.

The church at Schocklach

Overton Hall farm

This is a well-known producer of farmhouse cheese which can be purchased in Malpas and Whitchurch. The ancient hall dates back several centuries as does the craft of cheese making.

Malpas

Marches Way brings the walker first to the impressive church of Malpas, standing on a little knoll above the market square. Historians suggest that the site has been occupied by a church for many centuries but the one we see dates mainly from the latter part of the 14th century. It contains several tombstones and artefacts associated with the Brereton and Cholmondeley families and is well worth viewing. Nearby stands a castle mound but no stonework remains. The small town retains its medieval layout, a reflection of its importance as a borough and market centre. The town is on the Cheshire Cycleway, a way-marked route through the back lanes of Cheshire.

Cheese Making

The southern reaches of Cheshire and northern flanks of Shropshire are renowned for their cheesemaking. Whitchurch was very much a centre for cheese production in years gone by, shipping it out by the train load. The art (or science) of cheese making is still practiced on several farms in this area and farmhouse cheese is as different again from processed cheese.

The farmhouse white or red cheshire is popular in local markets with a crumbly texture and salty taste. Connoisseurs go for the matured Cheshire or Shropshire Blue. Look out for them when asking for your next plough-

Cheese making (Courtesy of Genus)

man's lunch. Farther south, traditional cheese is now also being made at Caerphilly.

REFRESHMENT

The Bull at Shocklach is a friendly old pub which opens daily from noon until three and then at 7 pm again in the evenings. Food is also served every day except Mondays and the pub serves a fine pint of draught Burtonwood and Bass beers.

Malpas has several inns. The most famous is **The Red Lion**, a Good Beer Guide entry for several years which is open all day throughout the week and usual hours on Sundays, offering Drawwell/Hanby ales from Wem. Food is served and accommodation is available (0948)860368. James I stayed at the inn in 1624 and the very chair where he sat survives – but don't sit on it, for there's a local custom that those who do should buy the bar a round.

The **Vaults Inn** opposite the church is also open throughout the day except Wednesday afternoons when the pub opens at 5 pm. Sunday times as usual. Food is served and the draught beer is John Smith's Traditional. There's also The Crown public house is nearby, so the walker need not go thirsty.

There is also a popular restaurant in the centre.

ACCOMMODATION

The Red Lion at Malpas and also bed and breakfast accommodation.

PUBLIC TRANSPORT

There is a regular service to Whitchurch and slightly less frequent to Chester on Mondays to Saturdays. Contact Cheshire Busline on (0244) 602666 for details.

THE WALK

1. Before the bridge leading to Wales and the village of Holt, go left to pass by a picnic site and restaurant, along a track which soon becomes a riverside path with views across the waters of the Dee to the remains of Holt castle. The path follows the river to an underbridge carrying the A534 road and then proceeds through another field to cross a stile.

2. The marker for a local walk indicates to go left, but you bear right to follow the river meander to the remains of a scrubbed hedge with only a few trees surviving. Turn left here and follow the line of the old hedge. Walk on the right of the old hedge to join a track a little farther along, a lane full of brightly coloured butterflies in summer. This climbs up a gentle bank to become a wider track and through very large gates by a silage storage area so now is a good time to hold your nose.

3. At the road go right to pass by the entrance to Crewe Hall, Laurel Bank Oak Furniture and soon by Crewe Bank farm. The road becomes a rough track which leads into a small field. Go ahead through a gateway still with the hedge on the right and continue towards the field corner but seeking a stile just to the left. Cross this and keep ahead, with Caldecott farm to the left, to cross another stile leading into a long and narrow enclosure. Go right and as this begins to descend the bank as a narrow track, go left through a stile by a gate.

4. Walk ahead to pass the head of a gully on the right and then bear slightly right to a hedge corner just to the right of a barred gate. At the corner, proceed ahead to a stile which is crossed. Bear slightly right across the next field and cross another stile and ditch crossing. Keep in the same direction through two more fields, the stiles being easy to locate. Then bear left along the field edge to cross a stile. Bear slightly right across this next field but keep to the left of the pool, the stile being in the hedge on the left. Once over, keep ahead through a gap in the next boundary and on to a sleeper bridge and stile by a large ditch at the field corner. Cross both and bend slightly left to cross a stile by a gate in wet ground, known to be flooded by the Dee on occasion. Proceed ahead through another pasture and look for a stile in the hedge near to the far corner. Cross it.

5. See a bridge ahead. This is the line of the path which continues to meet another path at the trees by an extruding field corner. Walkers should proceed to this point and retrace steps back to a stile in the hedge on the left. In reality, most walkers simply follow the hedge on the left to a stile which is crossed. In the next field, head diagonally across the field to a stile in the top far corner.

6. Cross the lane and a stile. Then walk diagonally through the enclosure to cross another stile. Walk through the churchyard to the northern gate onto the road. Turn right and as the road bears left keep ahead to cross a stile behind a small brick building. Keep ahead to cross the next boundary fence between two tall oaks and then ahead with the hedge on the right. Head for a stile by a gate into the next boundary, the houses of Shocklach now coming into view. Go through it and the path continues across the field. Look for a stile leading into the small field with a cottage on the left and cross slightly right to exit onto a road known as Green Lane, by a footpath signpost.

7. Bear left and walk into the village, passing the school and a telephone kiosk. Turn right and then left by The Bull Inn and ahead at the next junction. Pass by The Manor Farm and a track leading off right before looking for a stile opposite a bungalow. At the end of the field go through a gate and then bear left, the hedge now being on your left. Go through another gate and keep ahead to a gated bridge. Cross this and another ditch, then follow the line of a hedge slightly left through grazing pasture. Cross a narrow green enclosure and a stile into the next

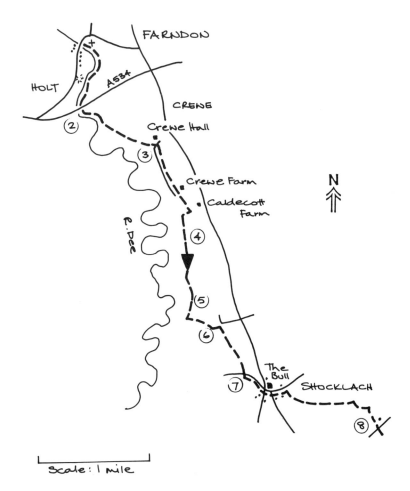

field heading slightly right to join the far hedge by a wood. Pass by a pool and then cross the field boundary and turn right to walk ahead to a small gate. Go through this and walk ahead to a far hedge. Bear left and walk ahead, turning right over a stile just before a water trough. Go straight on through this field to exit by way of a gateway onto a road by a house.

8. Turn left and then right, following a hedge on the left until a gap and then ahead on the right to a house where a stile is crossed. Go over a road and cross another stile. Head up the field, bearing slightly left to a corner and then slightly left again to a stile which stands to the right of a wood. Cross it and another shortly afterwards, then walk towards the handsome Chorlton Hall bearing slightly right across the parkland towards fencing, where there is a gate leading onto a drive. Bear right but at the fork go left (avoiding the drive to the main entrance) and very shortly cross a stile on the left. Proceed down the bank, heading for the top far left corner where there is a gate. Go through it and follow the stream now on the right up the valley and to a wicket gate leading to a bridleway.

9. Go right to pass behind Overton Hall, one of Cheshire's fine cheese making farms, going through several gates. Keep ahead along the way, the first part being used for access to fields but then proceed ahead along a narrower, shaded section which can become wet in winter months. This soon brings the walker to a minor road at Overton Heath.

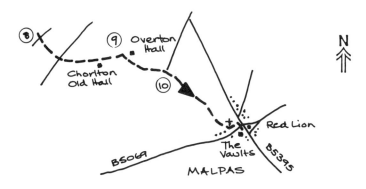

10. Bear right along the road and follow it up the hill but half way up look for a stile and signpost on the right. Walk up the steps and proceed to another stile. Make your way ahead along a well used path leading to Malpas, with great views across to the hills of Wales. Cross another stile and approach houses but bear left to cross another stile by a gate to walk along a back lane to Malpas church, a landmark for miles around and a fine way to enter this Marches town.

Malpas Church

MALPAS TO WHITCHURCH

START: Malpas Church

DISTANCE: 13 km (8 mls)

MAPS: Pathfinder Sheet 807, Whitchurch and Malpas

ROUTE DESCRIPTION

The route rises over the northern flank of Goodmoor Rough to descend into the snug of Bradley Brook. It climbs once again through meadows to Tushingham and onto the Llangollen branch of the Shropshire Union Canal, having joined the Sandstone Trail. Marches Way leaves the towpath at Dansons Bridge along a well-worn path through several small enclosures *en route* to Whitchurch.

Llangollen Canal, near Whitchurch

FEATURES

Tushingham Church and Chapel

Tushingham church on the main A41 road, is a fine looking building dating from the 1860s. A little farther on, however, is the gem, Saint Chad's Chapel. This stands forlorn in a field with no road access. The little brick chapel was built to serve Tushingham Hall and its local population when it was considered too far to walk to Malpas on the sabbath. The chapel was rebuilt in the late 1680s and inside there are surviving pieces of furniture from the seventeenth century.

Grindley Brook

The flight of locks at Grindley Brook offers a place to rest awhile, and to watch the novice boaters negotiate their way from lock to lock, attempting all manner of manoeuvres – much to the annoyance of the lock keeper.

Whitchurch

The medieval gate names – Bluegates, Bargates and Watergate – underline the importance of Whitchurch as an early border settlement. While the street pattern remains, the surviving architecture dates mainly from Georgian times and the walker will find information about the town on some of these buildings. The church of Saint Alkmund stands gauntly at the top of High Street, a rebuild of an earlier church which almost collapsed after Evensong one day in 1711, which says something for the singing in those days. It is said that two Shakespearian characters, Sir John Talbot, mentioned as the scourge of France in Henry IV, and Sir Henry Percy, known as Hotspur, were brought to rest here. The latter had his body exhumed to display at Shrewsbury Castle as evidence to the townsfolk that he had been slain.

Whitchurch has a market on Friday but the town is a busy centre on most days.

REFRESHMENT

Marches Way passes the **Willey Moor Lock Tavern** at Willey Moor lock. There is also a short diversion to the ancient **Blue Bell Inn** at

Tushingham, half a mile along Willey Moor lane from the route. At Grindley Brook there is a shop and **The Horse and Jockey** public house on the main road. The pub opens from noon until 3 pm on Mondays to Saturdays and from 7 pm in the evening (Usual hours on Sunday). It serves Banks mild and bitter on draught, also food.

Whitchurch has several of cafes, take-away food premises and a goodly number of taverns to choose from.

ACCOMMODATION

Accommodation is available in Grindley Brook and Whitchurch.

PUBLIC TRANSPORT

Buses serving Malpas and Whitchurch pass Grindley Brook. Contact Cheshire Bus on (0244) 602666 for details.

THE WALK

1. From Malpas church turn left into the market place and then right to pass the Crown and The Red Lion public houses in Old Hall Street.

2. Turn left after a garage into Springfield Road and then next right into Springfield Avenue. This residential road curves left but look for a track on the right between houses leading to garages. Go between two of them to cross a stile and head straight across the field towards a pool, with a small works beyond. Cross a stile by a gate and walk ahead again away from the stream and towards the hillock to your left, known as Goodmoor Rough.

Walk with a fence on the right and the path joins a discernible track leading gently along the hillside. At the end of the first section of this worn track, at a field boundary before the hillside really begins, go left up the hill following a hedge on the left. At the top move away from the hedge towards wooden fencing by a gate. Cross this and keep company with the hedge on the right. Follow it to the corner and bear slightly right across a field to go through a gate and into a back road.

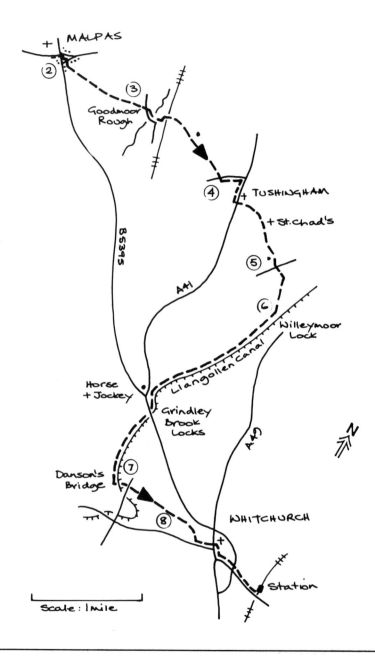

3. Turn right and the lane begins to curve left to descend into a trough, known as Bradley Brook. At the bottom corner go ahead over a stile and climb slightly left along a bank, with stream to the left, and then up to a gate. Go through it to scramble up onto the old railway trackbed where the path bears left through swathes of vetch, Rosebay Willow Herb, plantain and clover to a gate. Once through go right to head slightly left across a field with Millmoor farm just across the valley.

Go left near the fence to walk up to a barred gate. Go through it and now follow the hedge on the right up to the field corner near the farm. Just before the farm, go through a gate on the right and then bear left to walk up the hill past the farm and through a gate. Follow the hedge on the left ahead to a wicket gate and ahead again, following the hedge on the left as it tapers to a stile by a gate and exits onto a minor road.

4. Turn left and walk by houses up to the main A41 road. Go right to walk a short distance along the pavement, to Tushingham church. The path is signposted on the left through kissing gates and into a field at the rear of the car park.

Walk straight on to the edge of this short pasture, then head slightly right across the next field as waymarked on The Sandstone Trail, with the small chapel of Saint Chad's to your left. Cross the stile signposted to Grindley Brook and proceed ahead to the right of the chapel to cross another stile on the Sandstone Trail. Keep ahead down the next field to cross another stile. The path becomes a winding green track to a farm lane which passes to the left of the farm and then cuts off left to a stile onto a minor road.

5. Cross over and cross a stile, the way being signposted to Willey Moor Lock. Walk along the field edge on the right to another stile ahead and cross this. Then bear slightly left to the next stile. Once over keep company with the hedge on your left and follow it to another stile towards Moorhead farm. Keep ahead to cross a track and another stile. The path passes a small cottage and continues ahead to reach the Llangollen Canal towpath by the Willey Moor Lock public house.

6. Turn right and walk along this summertime navigation to Grindley Brook and then onwards for just less than a mile to Danson's Bridge. Walk up to and cross the bridge then keep ahead to the embankment of the new Whitchurch ring road to cross a stile by the access road to

Danson's farm, which can be seen on the left. Your way is down the access road to the main road. Cross the road with care and climb up the embankment on the other side to cross another stile.

7. Bear slightly right through the field, with a building to your left to cross a stile by a gate. Then keep slightly right again, heading up the field to a stile in the hedge to your right, mid-way up the field. In the next field the path bears slightly left over the brow of a hillock and to cross another stile. Proceed ahead to pass to the right of a derelict barn and the church of Saint Alkmund's can now be seen clearly.

8. The path drops to a double stile guarding a sleeper bridge and again bears slightly right through another small meadow to cross a stile in the right hand hedge. In the next field head in a direction slightly left of the church on the horizon to cross a stile in a tall hedge. The path bears right by a garden and then left across a field to cross yet another stile and sleeper bridge. It then heads slightly right again towards houses coming alongside a garden hedge through rougher ground.

Parish Church, Whitchurch

9. Pass by a garden, cross a road and keep ahead along a track and across a new bridge. Then follow the narrow path ahead and up steps on to Sherrymill Hill. Turn left and follow the road as it curves left into Yardington towards the church. Turn right to pass the church on your left and walk ahead into High Street. At the bottom of High Street go left into Green End. This crosses the main A41 road and continues ahead along Station Road to Whitchurch railway station.

WHITCHURCH TO WEM

START: Whitchurch Railway Station

DISTANCE: 18 km (11 mls)

MAPS: Pathfinder Sheets 807 Whitchurch and Malpas, 828 Ellesmere and Prees, and 848 Wem and Myddle

ROUTE DESCRIPTION

The route traverses mainly gentle pastures between the quiet rural settlements of Tilstock and Edstaton. The break in the tranquillity comes soon after Brown Moss nature reserve when the path crosses the busy A41 road at Prees Heath, packed with roadside eating places. There is a cut-off or start point at Prees railway station.

FEATURES

Brown Moss Nature Reserve

The name 'Moss' is something of a misnomer for there is little peat here today. It could well have been extracted throughout the centuries for fuel. The heathland and scrub areas are dotted with shallow pools, remnants from post glacial times when the great ice flows of the last Ice Age began to melt and flow away through the lowlands. These pools attract a wide range of birds including the great crested grebe and busy little reed bunting.

Tilstock

The old village of Tilstock has managed to retain its church dating from the 1830s, school, shop and post office, pub and even its own bowling and tennis club. Evidence of its importance as a farming centre can still be seen in the village.

Edstaton

Marches Way passes by the Norman church at Edstaton and several early pieces of distinctive architecture remain for the walker to see. It is said that George Bernard Shaw stayed in the locality on many occasions and despite his lack of reverence for religion was known to attend services at this church. To the right beyond the bus garage are the remains of the Prees Branch of the Shropshire Union canal and the old wharf and warehouses can still be seen. Built in the last years of the eighteenth century, this rural navigation survived until the end of the second world war. The section between Edstaton and Quina Brook was finally filled in during the 1970s.

Wem

Wem is home to the Sweet Pea Festival of Great Britain, a celebration of the work of Henry Eckford who developed the sweet pea as a highly scented bloom. Wem was chronicled in the Domesday Book and grew up as a walled town surrounding a castle and a church.

Sweet pea tribute to William Eckford (Courtesy of N. Shrops. District Council)

A great fire devastated the town in 1677 and much of the earlier settlement was destroyed although the street patterns remain. Since these times Wem has become a local market place (Market Day is Thursday) and during the past century enhanced by its brewing tradition. However, when Greenall Whitley closed the Wem Brewery in 1988 it was a sad loss to the town but the tradition continues with the production of Hanby Ales in the town, albeit on a smaller scale to the previous brewery.

REFRESHMENT

There are several cafes at Prees Heath and **The Horseshoes** pub at Tilstock. In Wem there are cafes and several inns to choose from although they sell mainly brews from the old Greenall Whitley empire. The town is well known for its speciality local foods such as the range of cheeses and breads available from T. O. Williams' shop on the High Street.

ACCOMMODATION

Accommodation is available at Prees Heath and at Wem.

PUBLIC TRANSPORT

There is a daily rail service between Whitchurch and Wem, allowing a day's walking between stations. There is also a station at a mid-way point along this section of the route at the very rural station of Prees.

THE WALK

1. From Whitchurch railway station entrance bear left and go left under the railway bridge. Cross the road and turn right past a house along a track by corrugated sheds and other buildings. The path bears left to pass to the rear of industrial premises, corralled between a fence and hedge. At the far end look for a stile on the right, cross it and proceed ahead. Go through a stile by a gateway and straight on again to another stile in the corner of the field which leads to a lane.

2. Turn left here to pass by cottages and up to the relief road. Cross with care. Follow the road opposite towards Edgeley but not far along, as the

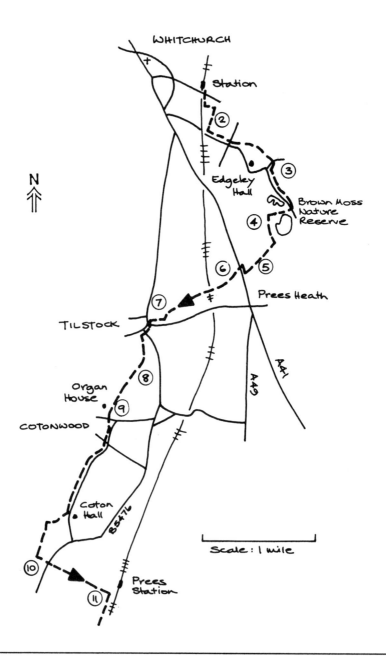

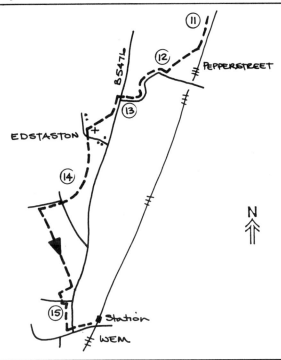

road bends right, bear left onto a bridle way as signposted. Proceed along the hedgerow on the left but as the hedge cuts off left go right across a field to a gate, with Edgeley Hall to the right. Keep ahead, however, towards a group of trees and to a barred gate leading onto a road. Turn right and at the junction by the houses bear left.

3. This road leads to Brown Moss nature reserve. Pass a picnic area and cottages on the left before turning right into a car parking area. Walk to the right of the Information Board along a broad green path, with the main pool to the left. It begins to head slightly right and then winds its way through young birch trees, soon to join another main path at the wood's edge, with a cottage to your right. Bear left and walk a short distance to a house on the right.

4. Just beyond it, cross a stile on the right and walk up the field's edge on your right. The field boundary is partly grubbed towards the field corner. Go through a gap between windswept hawthorns and cut slightly right across the next field to go through a gap in the hedge by an

electricity supply pole. In the next field, bear slightly left towards buildings and the noise of the busy A41 road at Prees Heath.

5. Cross a double bridge guarding a footbridge and proceed ahead along the hedge on the right to the road. Passage across this road is not easy so be vigilant for the traffic moves at a pace. Once across, turn right and very shortly pass a half timbered country cottage, with a date mark 1602, before turning left down a track to cross a stile by a gate.

6. Head slightly left over this large field to go through a gateway and then bear slightly right to cross a field and the railway line, so be careful. Once over, head slightly left across a field to cross a stile and continue ahead again in a similar direction towards the village of Tilstock. Cross another stile and proceed ahead again following a line of old trees as it curves gently to the left in a direction just to the left of the church tower. Cross a stile into a school playing field and walk alongside a fence to a stile leading onto a road. Go right.

7. Walk through the village keeping left at the first junction to pass by a shop, post office and telephone kiosk. Then go right at the junction by the Horseshoes public house. Pass by a farm and go left down a road marked with a "No Through Road" signpost. This passes by bungalows and houses away from the village and as it curves right keep ahead to cross a stile by a gate into a large field. Do not follow the track but bear slightly right across the field towards, but just keeping to the left of, a solitary oak tree.

8. Cross two stiles and a sleeper bridge and then bear slightly right to join a hedge on the right. Follow it for a few paces before cutting slightly left across the field to a stile half way along the hedge opposite. Go over the stile and bear left. Cross another stile and walk ahead through a narrow paddock to a gate. Go through it and keeping to the left of a pool to go through the hedge with a building, known as Organ House, on the right. At the far right corner of the next field a stile exits onto a drive. Turn left and walk a few paces down the drive to another track. Go right at the junction.

9. After a few paces cross a stile on the left and follow the path directly over a field to another stile ahead. Bear right and follow the road past a telephone kiosk and chapel in Cotonwood. Ignore all turnings to the left

or right until the entrance to Coton Hall is reached on the left. Turn right here to pass Coton Lodge and at the next triangular junction bear left and walk ahead to pass another junction and turning to the right. At the next junction a wider road is joined and the walker turns left.

10. This soon meets a junction with the main B5476 road. Walk over the road to a stile and cross it. Proceed through a small field to cross a double stile and then keep ahead to cross another double stile. To the left, in the distance, stands an old disused windmill – one of many which would have been found in this area in earlier times. Go straight on in the next field to cross a stile by a gate and then bear very slightly right to another stile, with Prees railway station now in sight. Cross this and walk ahead with a hedge to your right. Three quarters of the way down a stile cuts through the hedge and the walker continues to walk the remainder of the field on the other side of the hedge. Cross a stile by a gate leading onto a track. Those seeking a cut off point should bear left to pass by the signal box to the station.

11.Those continuing should turn right along the track and, as this begins to curve more sharply right, bear left through a gate and ahead to the fence by the railway embankment. Turn right to walk along it almost to the far end of the field but before reaching the tree lined stream bear right along a tractor track to cross the stream by way of a small bridge and gate. Keep ahead towards a gateway leading into the next field but just before bear left through a gap between a remnant of a hedge and water trough to join a low level fence, on your right. Follow it along the field's edge to a gateway.

12. Turn right on the road and walk up to a collection of farms known as Pepperstreet. Bear left at the junction and follow this narrow lane, passing by Edstaton Hall and farm to the main road once again. Cross over and bear left to walk the length of a field to a stile on the right. Cross it and walk ahead at first to a point parallel with a little bridge on the right. Then, head towards the right end of Edstaton church where a stile brings the walker to a road and to join The Shropshire Way. Turn left on the road.

13. At the corner, go right by a cottage, walking between a hedge and wire fencing to a garage. Cross a stile and bear left to proceed ahead across a large field, often in crop, to a stile in the far left corner. Cross

the stile and keep ahead in another large field, to pass to the left of a tree sheltered pool but then bear slightly right looking for a stile at a protruding corner of the field boundary. Cross the stile and keep ahead, hence cutting a corner, to another stile beneath a tree. Once over, go slightly left across a field corner to the next stile. Walk very slightly left through a pasture to another stile and then in the next field walk straight ahead, keeping company with a hedge on the right. The path exits onto a road by way of a stile by a gate.

14. Turn left and almost immediately right on the road signposted to Loppington. Pass by a farm on the left and not far beyond is a stile on the left, the route also being signposted. The path is well walked by people from nearby Wem so following the route is easy enough.

Proceed through three stiles in succession. Go through a gap and then keep ahead through another two stiles. After the second, walk with the hedge on your right. Within a short distance cross a stile on the right, then a sleeper bridge and go left. Cross a stile beneath an oak tree and proceed ahead once again towards modern housing. The path comes to a stile and garden fencing. This curves around to the right to a road. Keep ahead for a short distance before turning left along Trentham Road through a residential area. Turn left at the next main junction (not into cul de sacs) and continue ahead towards the Hawkstone Arms public house.

15. As you approach it, cross the road and turn right by a wall and holly hedge to walk down a narrow town path, known as Drawell Walk, by the old Wem Brewery (now Wem Business Park) and into High Street. Turn left for the railway station but right if continuing the route, then turn left before Wem church.

WEM TO YORTON

START: Wem Railway Station

DISTANCE: 9 Km (6 mls)

MAPS: Pathfinder Sheet 848, Wem and Myddle

ROUTE DESCRIPTION

The route leaves Wem along the banks of the River Roden to Tilley and then continues across arable and dairying pastures to the wooded slopes of Grinshill Hill and to Clive and Yorton.

FEATURES

Tilley

A pleasant village with several examples of half-timbered housing including Tilley Hall opposite to The Raven public house.

Grinshill Woods

This escarpment of sandstone and marl was once quarried for the construction of many local buildings in the neighbourhood and Shrewsbury. Grinshill sandstone is said to flank the doorway of Number 10 Downing Street, so check this when you next see the Prime Minister making a speech on the doorstep. In the 1970s part of the woodland was donated to Shropshire County Council and Corbet Wood nature trail is well loved by local people. Marches Way leads into the hamlet of Grinshill with several fine houses.

Clive

The spire of Clive church can be seen from miles around. The old buildings nearby, including Clive Hall, form part of a conservation area. The stone bottomed path leading up by the church entrance to the school is known locally as the Glat, simply meaning alley. Almost opposite is Blackhurst of Shropshire which offers oak smoked fish, poultry and venison free from artificial colourings and preservatives. The smoking process is carried out in a traditional smoke house and the smell is delicious.

REFRESHMENT

Refreshment is available at **The Raven** public house at Tilley and **The Elephant and Castle** at Grinshill. The latter is a fine old pub open from 11 a.m. until 3 p.m. on Mondays to Saturdays and from 6.30 p.m. in the evening. Food is available as is draught bass and sometimes another guest beer. Accommodation is also available (93 928) 410. Clive has a shop but no public house. **The Railway Inn** near to Yorton station is a good place to rest before the train arrives but tends not to open at lunchtimes.

ACCOMMODATION

Wem or Myddle (see next chapter)

PUBLIC TRANSPORT

Clive is served by a local Wem to Shrewbury bus service on Monday to Saturday. Yorton has a Monday to Saturday train service between Wem and Shrewsbury.

THE WALK

1. From Wem railway station, turn left to walk down Aston street and High Street. At the junction just before the church turn left to walk down Mill Street to a point opposite Wem mill where a track, signposted to Tilley, leads off to the right alongside the banks of the River Roden. The track gives out by a cottage into a field and then a well worn path follows the river to a tractor bridge which is crossed. The path continues alongside a tributary brook rather than the farm track and exits through a kissing gate onto a road.

2. Turn left to walk through the village of Tilley, with several half-timbered houses and a pub, The Raven to welcome the visitor. As the road bends left keep ahead along a No Through Road to cross the railway at unmanned crossing gates with extreme caution.

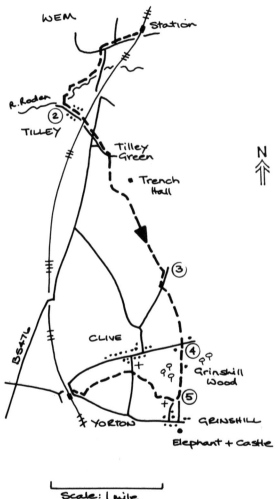

Scale: 1 mile

Proceed ahead to cross the main B5476 road and continue along a narrow lane opposite, signposted to Tilley Green, a most charming name for a rural settlement. Pass by houses and shortly, a lane comes from the right but keep ahead. At the corner as the road bears left continue ahead up a No Through Road. Join the Shropshire Way by a house as the path bears right to cross a stile into a small field.

Cross a stile and then head very slightly left across a large field, with Trench Hall and farm standing to the left, one time home of writer John Ireland. Cross the next stile and part-way up the field cross another stile. Then continue to proceed ahead but with the hedge now on your right. This tends to be dairying country and often those irritating little electric fences (which stop the cows chewing everything in sight) have to be crossed in some fields. The way is ahead through several fields until a stile exits into a green lane where the walker turns right.

Quarrying

The sandstone quarried at Grinshill was, at one time, much in demand and orders were received from as far away as the USA. Sandstone has been hewn from hillsides throughout The Marches. Small-scale quarries extracting the rich red sandstone for building purposes can also be seen in Herefordshire and Gwent. Other areas, such as Mortimer's Forest and the Lugg plains yield limestone and conglomerate aggregates for building purposes. Not all welcome these extractions and many local communities have fought to conserve their special landscapes but the quarrying interests more than often win permission to develop the sites regardless.

3. Within a short distance go left as signposted to cut through the top edge of a field before crossing two stiles by an enclosed pond and then ahead again with the hedge to the right once again. keep ahead to cross a track and another stile and then bear slightly left towards the top left corner of the field. Cross a stile and footbridge and then keep ahead to a stile in the corner onto a road.

4. Go right but then very shortly left to cross a stile leading into a field. At the corner go right over a stile by a gate and then bear left to continue up the hill and to cross a stile by a cottage. Go through a small enclosure to cross another stile and cross a track to bear slightly left down a narrow path dipping down

through Grinshill wood. Keep to the left as the path drops to join a sunken track below, used in previous times to cart away stone. Then go right to follow this down through a wood to Grinshill village. The track comes to an old village hall. Bear left for a diversion to the church and Elephant and Castle public house.

5. Otherwise when passing the village hall bear right by the Jubilee Oak, a fine specimen planted by Miss Cynthia Bibby in 1935. The way rises up along a sandstone trail linking houses nestled beneath the shelter of the bluff (known as The Cliffe) and soon comes to Clive Church with its tall spire, a landmark for some miles. Cross the minor road to walk down a lane almost opposite, towards the village club. After the house beyond it, look for a track leading to the left which soon reaches a gate and fields. Head down to the bottom right corner of the field and go through a gateway and then over a stile ahead. Continue almost ahead to a gate and onto a minor road.

6. Bear right to pass by a cut-off point, Yorton Station, or wander down to The Railway Inn, a place of refreshment enjoyed by many a weary rail traveller ending a journey after a day in town.

YORTON TO SHREWSBURY

START: Yorton Railway Station

DISTANCE: 19km (12 mls)

MAPS: Pathfinder Sheets 848 Wem and Myddle and 869 Shrewsbury

ROUTE DESCRIPTION

The walk is mainly through gently undulating farmland punctuated by a ridge of sandstone between Harmer Hill and Myddle. Following a track through to Merrington, the route then crosses fields to Bomere Heath and onwards through mixed farming country to the very outskirts of Shrewsbury at Coton Hill.

FEATURES

Myddle

The village of Myddle has been made famous by the outstanding work of Richard Gough who, at an old age, penned a social history based on those who attended the parish church in the latter part of the seventeenth century. Near to Myddle church stand the scant ruins of Myddle castle now surrounded by a farm.

Merrington

Marches Way passes Merrington Green, a common with little or no grazing now, hence the predominance of scrub woodland. Clay was evidently extracted from the Green for a local pit and brick works. There is a nature trail through the reserve.

Bomere Heath

This mainly dormitory village grew up around a common which no longer exists.

Shrewsbury

Shrewsbury has much to offer the visitor including the castle, abbey, several museums and walking tours from the Tourist Information centre, including some which follow in the footsteps of Brother Cadfael, the medieval monk who solved many a mystery. Some of the stories are based on Shrewsbury haunts. The Tudor and Georgian architecture, the back alleys known as Shuts and the compact nature of the town make it ideal for exploring on foot. This is definitely a place to stay awhile.

REFRESHMENT

The Red Lion at Myddle is open from 11 a.m. until 2.30 p.m Monday to Saturday and from 7 p.m. in the evening, serving Banks's Cask beers and food. The pub is a partly converted barn dating from the mid C17th and is full of character. There are many cafes and inns at Shrewsbury. **The Red Lion** at Bomere Heath is open from 11.30 a.m. until 3 p.m. Monday to Saturday and from 6.30 p.m. of an evening. This congenial local sells Davenports Traditional Mild and Tetley beer as well as food. Both pubs are open the usual hours on Sundays.

ACCOMMODATION

Accommodation is available at Myddle and Shrewsbury.

PUBLIC TRANSPORT

There are buses from Myddle and Bomere Heath to Shrewsbury on Monday to Saturday, should the walker feel like a break. Contact Shropshire Bus on (0345) 056785 for details.

THE WALK

1. From Yorton railway station bear left and then left again to walk through an underbridge and up to a road junction by houses. By the furthermost house on the right in the row walk between gardens, with overhanging fruit trees, as signposted. The path leads to a field where the walker continues along the right hand field hedge to a stile in the top right corner. Walk alongside the hedge on the right and still climbing cross a stile before a tree and then turn immediately left through a gap. The path now continues ahead with a hedge to the left to cross a stile and to the main B5476 road.

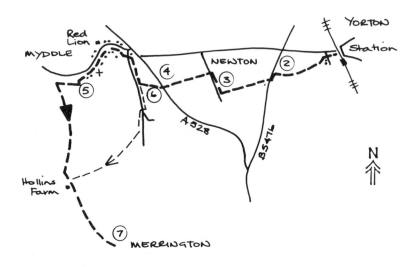

2. Cross the road and turn left to walk around the corner to a stile on the right, go over the stile. In the field, go ahead to an indent in the opposite hedge where bushes hide a sleeper bridge and stile. Cross both and keep ahead with a hedge on the right. This brings the walker to a stile on the right by a water trough and to a track curving gently into the hamlet of Newton on the Hill, the one-time home of writer Richard Gough.

3. At the road go right and walk past a farm and around a corner to a path which cuts left before a house, through a small belt of trees and into a field. Go right and follow the hedge to a stile by a gate. Keep company with a hedge on the right and to meet a little iron gate. In the next large field, the way is ahead to walk to the left of a clump of trees where this path is joined by another and then ahead to a gate.

4. Cross the main B5476 road and head slightly right across the field to the wood's edge. Shortly, cross a stile leading into the wood and a clear but narrow path leads between trees down to a minor road. Turn right and walk towards the village. Ignore the first signpost and stile on the left leading into a meadow but as road climbs up to houses in Myddle look for a little link path on the left (signposted) and follow this through to another road. Bear left and pass by the post office, the Red Lion pub, the school and church.

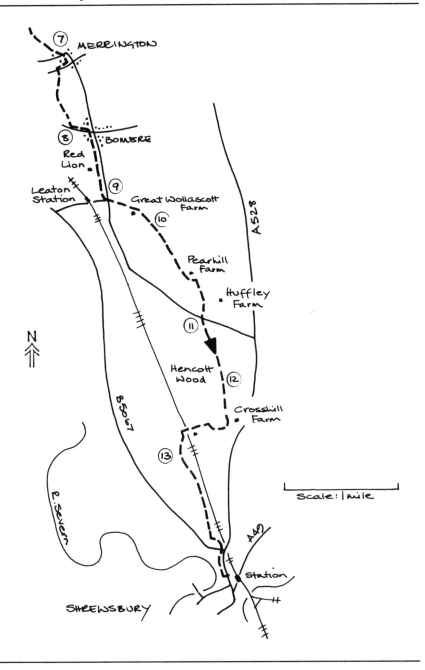

5. As the road leaves the village go through a gate on the left, the path being signposted and bear right across a field to join a field corner. Follow the hedge and fencing on the right to a footbridge and stile onto a track. Go left here and follow this for a mile to Merrington, passing Hollins farm half way along on the right.

6. A shorter route to Merrington (avoiding Myddle) from the B5476 is to keep ahead in the field to a small gate and steps down into a gully. The path widens into a track between red sandstone quarried areas, passing a cottage on the right before reaching a road. Go left and at the next junction bear right. In a short distance, turn right along a farm track to Webscott farm.

The track skirts the outbuildings and then before the farmhouse turns left to leave the farm buildings through a group of low lying fields. Pass by a group of yew trees and the track curves left. Look for a small gate on the right. Go through it and head slightly left across two fields going through another bridle gate. At the third gate the path comes to a lane by a farm known as The Hollins, where the main route is joined. Turn left and follow this track into the hamlet of Merrington, there being a nature reserve on the right of the track along the final section leading to the hamlet.

7. At the road continue the short distance ahead to a cross roads where a village pump and memorial to Robert and Elizabeth Salney dating from 1864 stands: a token of true appreciation from the community for their good deeds but, in particular, from Thomas and Elizabeth Eyton. Turn right here along a track over a brow and ahead. Just past a fine house on the right look for a gateway on the left leading into a field.

Walk across the field to a protruding corner on slightly elevated ground. Cross a stile here and bear right across the field, heading for an oak tree in the far hedge. Cross the fence here and before a pool turn left to follow the hedge on the left until it drops away left. Keep ahead to cross another stile. Head slightly right to go through a broken hedge and then join a track leading to a gate and a road in the village of Bomere.

8. Turn left and pass by more than one old chapel before turning right into Shrewsbury Road. Continue along this road out of the village towards the railway line as far as a road junction with a turning to the right to the old Leaton station.

9. Go left at this T junction, through a gap by a wooden bar and head slightly right across the field between large and small electric telegraph poles to a stile beneath a tree. Cross this and in the next field head towards a barn belonging to great Wollascott farm. Keep ahead to a junction and then bear right to walk on the outer perimeter of the farm buildings. This section is subject to improvement so please follow the waymarks as the path leaves the farm buildings back into fields. This should lead into a field with electricity pylons.

10. Proceed through this field beneath the pylons to a stile shaded by a tree. Then head very slightly right between the wires and a wood on the right to look for a stile (not immediately seen) in a thick hedge. Cross it and a ditch to join a very large field where the walker heads in a direction just to the right of Pearhill farm. Meet a field corner and keep ahead with the hedge on the right to the next field boundary.

Cross here and, in the next field, bear slightly left between the oak trees and look for a small gate. Go through this and then to a point in front of Pearhill farm (on the left), where the path turns right to cross a small field to a stile to the left of a tree. Keep ahead to pass to the right of a trim hedge with Huffley farm on the left and continue towards a field corner and onto a road by way of a stile.

11. On the other side, cross a stile and the path bears left to the remains of a grubbed hedge where a stile once stood. Just beyond bear left here to cross a stile and enter an expansive field where your way is slightly right between two oak trees and two electric telegraph poles and towards the left end of Hencott wood. Cross the boundary through a gap by the wood, a gap often overgrown in summer with bracken. In the next field the path bears right to follow the fields edge around for a 100 paces or so to a dip by the wood and through a gap in a hedge into another large field.

12. Head slightly right across the field, parallel with the hedge on the left at first but then bearing slightly right as the hedge drops away to the left. Cross a stile in the first field boundary and proceed ahead to another stile which leads the walker into a field situated to the right of Crosshill farm. Pass to the right of a pond and keep ahead to a stile (by metal fencing) which leads onto a lane. Go right and follow this past a farm and over a railway bridge. Go left, cross a stile by a gate, and

follow the green lane as it curves right along a bluff but shortly look for a stile left. Head down the field.

13. At the bottom of the field the path bears left towards the embankment to cross another stile and walk up the bank with the railway on the left. Cross another stile and keep ahead to cross another stile. Then shortly cut left to a stile by an old farm and walk up the drive (Corporation Lane) to a junction. Turn left at the road, Coton Crescent and then, at the end, bear left and almost immediately right into Coton Hill to descend alongside the River Severn to Chester Street. Bear left to walk under the railway bridge, then turn right for Shrewsbury railway station.

Shrewsbury – floral baskets adorn medieval cottages on Fish Street
(Shrewsbury Borough Council)

SHREWSBURY TO PONTESBURY

START: Shrewsbury Railway Station

DISTANCE: 16 km (10 mls)

MAPS: Pathfinder sheets 869 Shrewsbury and 889 Dorrington and Cressage

ROUTE DESCRIPTION

After two miles of town walking, the route follows the Rea Brook to Hook-a-Gate, then saunters through gentle farming country to Longden. From here, it climbs through very pleasant valleys and woodlands to the foot of Pontesford hill and into the large village of Pontesbury.

FEATURES

Hook-a-Gate

This unusual name is said to date from Anglo Saxon times meaning an enclosure of oak trees where deer were sometimes herded. There used to be a spa water supply bottled here but this is no longer in production.

Longden

The small village of Longden offers a cut off point for Shrewsbury.

Pontesbury

Pontesbury was at one time a local mining and agricultural settlement but is now very much a dormitory settlement for Shrewsbury. The village fans out from the impressive Saint George's church dating originally from the 12th century, but heavily restored since then.

Perhaps, Pontesbury's greatest claim to fame is that Shropshire author Mary Webb lived here. Landmarks such as the weird shaped outcrops of The Stiperstones feature in "The Golden Arrow" and other rural Shropshire scenes are written into "Gone to Earth" and "Precious Bane".

She loved Shropshire dearly and this is reflected in most of her works. It is unfortunate that Mary Webb's life was bedevilled by illness and she was only to receive acclaim after her premature death in the 1920s.

REFRESHMENT

The **Tankerville Arms** at Longden and **The Red Lion** at Pontesbury are at your service.

ACCOMMODATION

There is limited accommodation in the Pontesbury area.

PUBLIC TRANSPORT

Longden is served by bus on Monday to Saturday but the service to Pontesbury is more frequent. Contact Shropshire Busline on (0345) 056785.

THE WALK

1. From Shrewsbury railway station entrance turn left up Castle Gates which leads into Castle Street, a one way traffic route packed with cars. The route, however leads the walker to the pedestrianised Pride Hill enlivened by buskers playing for the shoppers. At the bottom, turn left into High Street and right into Market Square to pass by the Market Hall to the Tourist Information Centre in Market Street. A few paces along, bear left into Swan Hill and continue along it to a crossroads by the High School.

2. Pass by the school to descend to the Kingsland toll bridge across the Severn. There's a charge of 1p for cyclists and pedestrians, so have the change ready! The road bears left and then right before an overbridge. Bear left up steps here to join the road above, known as Canonbury. Turn left and follow the road as it bends right through this pleasant residential quarter.

Cross Kingsland road to Beehive lane and walk ahead, soon to meet another path coming in from the right. Your way descends through a partly cultivated pocket of land, in the valley of the Rad Brook, to rise once again to a main road, along a path known as the Cinder Path.

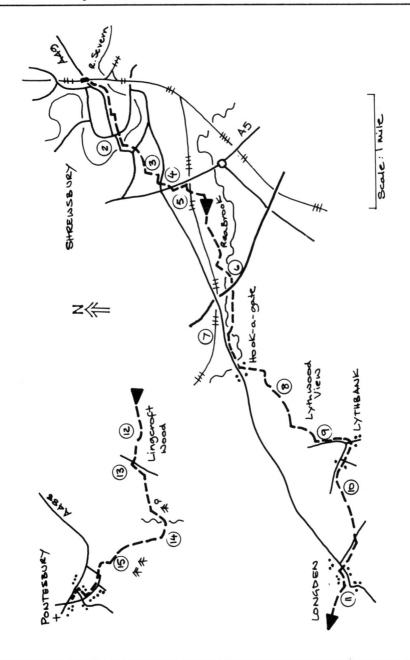

3. Cross the road and turn right to walk along the main Longden road to a point just beyond the entrance to a cemetery. Bear left here along a narrow link path to the main A5, Roman road, which is very busy, so care is needed to cross this.

4. Once over the Roman road, turn left and walk along the pavement for a short distance before turning right down a narrow path onto the edge of a playing field. There is a glimpse of the Shropshire hills beckoning but a mile or so of town walking to encounter yet. The path follows the perimeter fence left until it cuts left across the railway track of the Shrewsbury to Aberystwyth line.

5. The path passes between gardens and exits on Meole Walk. Bear left and then next right into Vicarage Road. Continue into Station road and then turn left along Alexandra Avenue which continues into Washford Road and more modern housing. This long road eventually curves right around a corner where a stile on the other side of the road enters fields. This corralled footpath leads into the open countryside of the Rea Valley, disturbed only by the noise of the ring road.

6. It brings the walker to a footbridge over the brook and then ahead for a few metres before bearing slightly right towards a bridge under the new road. Go under this and the path proceeds along the river bank for a little longer before climbing to the field's edge. Keep ahead along a well worn path to exit by way of a gap near gorse bushes and then bear right at the fork, climbing gently to a track. Go right here.

7. Turn left at the main road and walk, facing the traffic through the village of Hook-a-Gate. Before the telephone kiosk and school bear left to pass by a cottage to cross a stile almost adjacent to the school. Climb into a field beyond and follow the path by the stream on the left up to another stile. Cross this and continue ahead to a point where the boundary hedge curves sharp left and where a small gate is situated, an access point for another path joining from the Bayston Hill direction. Do not go through it but instead bear slightly right across the field at this point towards a stile next to a gate in the opposite hedge.

8. Once over the stile, keep company with the hedge on your left for the entire length of the field. This leads to a path (often hidden by bushes) which winds into a gully. Climb the opposite bank and in the next field

keep ahead to cross another fence. Then head very slightly right but keeping to the left of three oak trees to a corner where an old green track leads off left. This, believe it or not, is the right of way. However, you might note waymarks offering a permissive path which is far more viable. Before the gully, bear right for a short walk to a concrete track bridge. Go left here and cross a stile by a gate. Continue ahead with a hedge on your left and cross fencing into the next field. Head very slightly left between a pool and three oak trees to the old green track. The first section of this can get overgrown but some walkers simply walk along the field's edge to join the track a little farther along. The track then curves right and left towards Lythwood View. This joins an access track to the farm and your way is to the right down to a metalled road.

9. Turn left here for a short climb towards Lythbank but at the triangular junction bear right to descend once more to pass a junction, farm and cottage. Not far beyond is a path on the left, which is signposted. Cross a stile by a gate and through the coral before following a wooden fence on the right. Continue through a gate and keep ahead in the same direction towards a signpost and onto a road.

10. Cross the road, go through a gateway and proceed ahead to cross a stile to a much larger field. Walk in a similar direction but easing more gently left to a stile in a hedge. The stile is not easily seen at first. Once over, cut across the next field slightly left to a gateway onto a road. Go right for the short walk into Longden. At the main road turn left to pass by the telephone kiosk, garage, post office cum stores and The Tankerville Arms.

11. Just beyond the pub on the corner, bear right along Manor Lane and then look for a track on the right rather than dipping down into the housing. Follow the track into open countryside once again but as the main track continues to descend bear right along a rougher way between a wood and large hedge. This soon gives out at a stile into a field. Keep company with a hedge to your left as the path climbs this gentle and secluded valley, a rather pleasant spot. Cross another stile and a series of gates where sheep are herded by a pool.

12. Continue ahead up the dry valley with woodland on either side until you have nearly reached the top of the rounded enclosure. However, go

through the gateway on the right and then through a wicket gate on the left. The path soon reaches a pool and cuts to the left of it through gentle gorse banks. It joins another path and then bears right through scrub woodland to re-enter the field once again (some local walkers simply follow the pool's edge to reach the same point). Turn left and walk to a small gate into Lingcroft wood and near to another but larger pool, glimpsed through thick cover. The path brings the walker to a field where it continues ahead to a stile leading onto a metalled lane.

13. Turn left and pass by houses. The road bends to the left and then rises again. Bear right here along a track which climbs between high hedges. It descends by cottages and a house to woodlands and the beautiful valley of the Pontesford brook. Look for a narrow path cutting off left into the valley. Follow this down into the valley. Ignore the footpath sign indicating a way to the right but continue ahead to ford the stream. The path climbs again through soft shades of green to Earls Hill Barn on your left, a centre used by the Wildlife Trust.

14. Keep ahead, however, to a gate and follow the path as it winds around to another gate. Continue along what is now a more definable track to yet another gate and, as it descends gently, look out for a stile ahead, almost hidden, at the sharp right corner. Head for an electric telegraph pole in the field and not far beyond is a stile beneath a tree on the corner of a tall hedge. Cross the stile and bear right for Pontesbury. Those not calling at Pontesbury should see instruction 16.

15. The path soon descends to a road. Bear right and then turn left to walk along a drive. Before the building go right over a stile and across a well worn path over a field. This comes to a lane. Turn right and walk to the Mary Webb Comprehensive school. Turn left to pass by the school and library. At the end of the road turn right and at the main road left to walk by The Red Lion public house. Buses to Shrewsbury leave on the other side of the road.

16. For those not stopping at Pontesbury turn left and follow the path through the wooded slopes of Pontesford and Earl's Hill as explained in paragraph 1 of the next section.

PONTESBURY TO CHURCH STRETTON

START: The Red Lion, Pontesbury

DISTANCE: 19 km (12 mls)

MAPS: Pathfinder Sheets 889, Dorrington and Cressage and 910 Church Stretton

ROUTE DESCRIPTION

Walking through woodland beneath Earl's Hill, the route soon rises into Shropshire's best hill country. From Habberley, the route climbs the romantic Lawn Hill to Pulverbatch and then through remote sheep farming at Wilderley Hill. The route follows The Portway to The Long Mynd and descends Carding Mill valley to the outskirts of Church Stretton, a magnificent walk in good weather.

FEATURES

Pulverbatch

Marches Way passes another fine example of a motte and bailey castle on the way into Pulverbatch, a more important place in days gone by. The parish church in nearby Church Pulverbatch can be seen from the route when climbing away from Pulverbatch. This really is an unspoilt part of Shropshire.

The Portway

The ancient road, The Portway, dates from prehistoric times, when travellers kept to the high hills. The track has since been used by drovers throughout the centuries to bring cattle from the Welsh highlands to England to sell and now by walkers and horse riders.

The Long Mynd

This expanse of moorland broken up by deep ravines known locally as "batches" is now mainly in the care of the National Trust. The views over to Caer Caradoc and the Lawley are very inspiring.

Carding Mill Valley

This deeply incised valley is probably Shropshire's most popular countryside spot, spoilt only by the intrusion of cars in its upper reaches. The babbling brook flowing down the valley makes an ideal stop for a picnic.

Church Stretton

The small market town of Church Stretton also enjoys a reputation as a spa town and water is still bottled nearby for distribution throughout the land. Church Stretton did not quite reach the heights of popularity enjoyed elsewhere but the almost Alpine character, surrounded as it is by Caer Caradoc, Ragleth and The Long Mynd, is still very appealing.

Caer Caradoc from Marches Way, near Church Stretton

REFRESHMENT

The walk passes near **The Mytton Arms** at Habberley, which opens from 7 p.m. onwards every evening but at lunchtimes on the weekends from noon until 3 p.m. Brew 11 is on offer, an unusual beer for these parts. The Mytton Arms does not serve food.

Pulverbatch is fortunate in having two good pubs. **The White Horse** is open from 11 am until 3 pm, and from 7 pm in the evenings, serving Boddingtons, Marstons and Whitbreads Flowers Original on draught, as well as food. The landlord reminds us of an old ditty recited locally:

Cothercott upon the hill
Wilderley down in the dale
Churton for pretty girls
And Pulverbatch for good ale.

Nearby, **The Woodcock** opens at 7 pm on Monday to Friday, but also noon till 4 pm on Saturdays. Food is also available and the draught beers on offer are Bass and Stones Bitter. There's an old table in the pool room, whenever moved, tends to coincide with strange things happening such as clocks falling of the walls and the like so don't touch it. Both the White Horse and The Woodcock are open usual hours on Sunday.

A short diversion at Wilderley Hill takes the walker to the **Bottle and Glass** Inn at Picklescott, which is open from 11 am until 3 pm on Monday to Saturady and again at 7 pm. Marstons, Boddingtons and a guest beer are served on draught and food too in this old world inn dating originally from 1623. Usual Sunday hours. Accommodation is available. Tel: (069 45) 345.

There are several cafes and pubs to choose from in Church Stretton. A National Trust cafe is open during the summer months in Carding Mill valley.

ACCOMMODATION

Picklescott, just off the route.

Church Stretton offers a wide range of accommodation.

PUBLIC TRANSPORT

Buses serve the village of Pulverbatch (Monday to Saturday) for those wishing to return to Shrewsbury. Church Stretton is served by trains daily and there is a Monday to Saturday bus service to Shrewsbury. Contact Shropshire Busline for details on (0345) 056785.

THE WALK

1. From the Red Lion public house, near to Pontesbury church, turn right and almost immediately right again, then next left to pass through a housing area, by the library and the Mary Webb school. The road begins to curve left and opposite the school farmyard, not school yard, is a rough track leading off to the right. Follow this until it approaches Hill House farm where there is a stile on the left by a thorn bush.

Cross the stile and walk diagonally across the field to cross another stile. Once over, go left along a track until a metalled road is reached. Turn right to climb up to the access track on the left by the Forestry Commission sign for Pontesford Hill wood. This bears left into woodland. (Re-join Marches Way as indicated in paragraph 14 of the last section.)

2. The path climbs gradually through the woodland and then into a field. Keep ahead, still rising through the field to a gate leading into the Earl's Hill nature reserve, indicated by an information board. The path continues ahead through scrub and beneath the scree slopes of Earl's Hill. At the next fork bear left down to a wicket gate and into a large field. Bear slightly left, heading for a gate and ahead along the field hedge on your right.

Proceed through a gate and along a green track, with views over to a half timbered house and farm to the left. Shortly, look for a stile on the left which leads into a field. Cross the stile and go through a gate on the right. Bear slightly left along a hedge through rough ground to cross a stile into the next small field and head slightly right, to the right of the bungalow and garden, to another stile onto a metalled road. Those seeking refreshment should continue on the green track to reach the metalled road by a farm and turn right for the short walk to The Mytton Arms.

3. Once on the road, turn left and walk to the corner but bear right over a stile beneath the large oak tree on the right. Follow the hedge on the left ahead to the far field corner where a stile is crossed on the left. Go left over another stile in fencing and then bear right through a gate. Keep ahead through the field and through a gateway. Bear slightly left' across the next field to a footbridge, then walk through the next small

field to cross a stile which is easily seen. Join a tractor track at the bottom of the lower slopes of Lawn Hill, festooned with bracken.

4. The path curves to the left and climbs the batch between Lawn and Huglith hills, with the hedge to your right. This is a strenuous climb rewarded fortunately by good views over the tumbling foothills of the Welsh borderlands. Towards the summit, go through a small gate, climb the last section to another gate on the right and then bear left through a barred gate – no doubt heaving a sigh of relief that it is downhill all of the way to Pulverbatch now. Follow the tractor track as it curves gently right through a field to exit onto a lane enclosed by high hedges. Turn left on the lane and follow this into the village of Pulverbatch passing by a motte and bailey mound on your right and by houses and a lane joining from the left. A few steps away is the White Horse public house, where buses leave for Shrewsbury.

5. The route continues to the right at the road junction by the White Horse, along the Bishops Castle road as it descends into a valley. Half way down look for a stile on the left. Cross this and walk through the small field to cross a footbridge and two more stiles into the next field. Head slightly left across the gentle climb to another stile and join a lane.

6. Bear left and walk approximately one hundred paces towards Lea farm on the left before crossing to go through a gateway on the right. Bear slightly left across this field made large by the grubbing of an old hedgerow, a few remaining trees marking the boundary. From this point walk ahead in a similar direction towards the field boundary looking for a stile, which is not immediately seen at first. There is a good view back to Church Pulverbatch from this point and to the castle mound in Pulverbatch.

7. Once over the stile, keep almost ahead to cross another stile then proceeding ahead to two stiles guarding a sleeper bridge. Sheppen farm stands to the right in the near distance.

From the sleeper bridge keep ahead for fifty paces before bearing slightly right to join a hedge leading up to a left hand corner of the field with The Beeches farm now in sight on the left. Cross a stile by a gate and go ahead to the next stile marked with a Shropshire Way waymark.

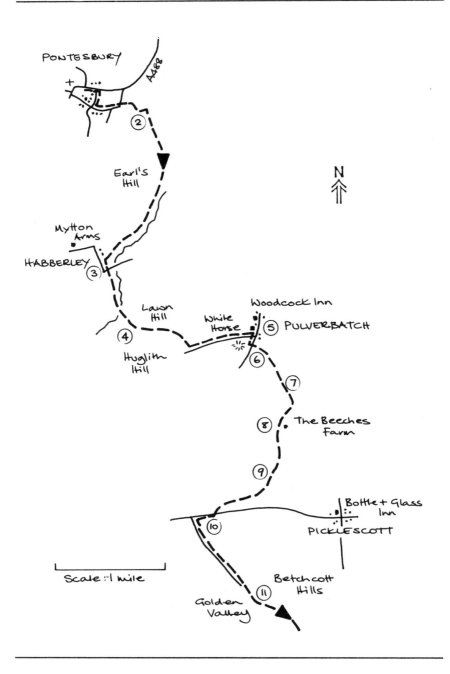

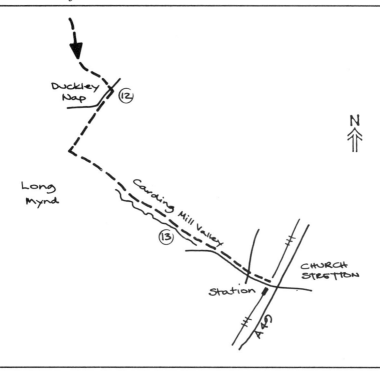

8. Cross the track and stile proceeding ahead a short distance to cross another stile. Once over bear right in the dip to proceed through the gateway and then head slightly left up the brow of a hillock, passing beneath electricity telegraph poles, and to the left of a double pole. There are fine views over to The Wrekin, one of Shropshire's favourite hills, a landmark seen for miles around. Cross the double stile and bridge bedded in the coniferous hedgerow to proceed through wet ground as the walker rises gently to the remains of a grubbed hedge. Keep to the right of this and as the brow of the hill is approached keep heading slightly right to a stile by a gate with the coniferous plantation just beyond.

9. Walk slightly left as the land continues to rise to another brow where it passes wet ground in a slight dip, with the plantation easing away to your right. Your way is to the top left hand corner where a stile leads onto a road. There's a good view to the right of Earl's Hill. Those seeking accommodation or refreshment at Picklescott should turn left here for the half mile walk to the hamlet.

Otherwise, once on the road, bear right for a very short distance and then turn left along a narrower tarmac lane, The Portway. Opposite in the field stands a memorial to T.J. Powys Esq, dated 1791.

10. The lane continues ahead for about half a mile and then the Shropshire Way bears off right, down Golden Valley towards the secluded hamlet of Ratlinghope. Your way, however, is to continue ahead through a gate and to climb the slopes of Betchcott hill. The Portway is now a green track, curving left through a gate by a barn, and a trig point beyond to the right.

11. At the end of this field it becomes a more definable track and easy to follow as it curves gently right along a ridge. Another track comes in from the right and there is a climb with the Darnford valley to the right. Proceed through gateways and then the track bears gently left, still climbing but then dipping finally before the last little climb up to a tarmac road.

12. Turn right and follow the road for a short distance until it bends right. Keep ahead here, at a point known as Duckley Knap. In the distance, to the right, the weird shapes of the Stiperstones can be seen. This main green track soon comes to a junction of paths on The Long Mynd. Your way is slightly left, descending from the moorland to a clear path, Motts Road, which drops into one of Shropshire's best-known coutryside haunts, the Carding Mill Valley.

13. Its popularity is hardly surprising, for the views over to Caer Caradoc and Ragleth hills are breathtaking, especially as the mist is rising on an autumn morning. Carding Mill valley also has a charm about it, despite cars being allowed so high up into the hills. Could this be a case for gently persuading countryside lovers to leave their vehicles farther down the valley? Your way takes you to this higher car park, over the ford and down to the National Trust shop and cafe, which is open throughout the summer months.

14. Walk a little farther down the road but then look for a path, which climbs slightly right up the hillside on the right once across the stream. This leads to the outskirts of Church Stretton at another road. Turn left and follow it down into town. Cross directly over by the Midland Bank and walk down Sandford Avenue to the railway station.

Earl's Hill, Pontesbury

CHURCH STRETTON TO CRAVEN ARMS

START: Church Stretton Railway Station

DISTANCE: 16 km (10 mls)

MAPS: Pathfinder Sheets 910 Church Stretton and 931 Craven Arms

ROUTE DESCRIPTION

Climbing out of Church Stretton to the flanks of Ragleth, the views are exceptional – as is the walk through Chelmick and Rag Batch to Acton Scott. Gently lies the route into Apedale but then it is a hard climb up to Wenlock Edge. Along the edge in a south westerly direction and then descend once again into the valleys of the Quinny and Onny, waters where often herons can be seen.

FEATURES

Acton Scott Historic Working Farm

Ploughing, sowing and harvesting are the perennial pastimes of all farmers but this splendid working farm illustrates life before the arrival of the tractor, or the internal combustion engine. It is not only the horses that make the place so atmospheric but activities such as butter making and other crafts. This place re-creates the conditions of an early upland Shropshire farm and is open daily from late March to late October.

Wenlock Edge

The long limestone ridge, made famous by A.E. Housman, stretches for about 15 miles from Much Wenlock to Craven Arms. It has been quarried in the past but thankfully not to a point of devastation and has most certainly been a walking route since the earliest of times.

Craven Arms

The small town of Craven Arms owes its existence to the sale of sheep and to a lesser extent this is still the case. It was the coming of the railway that made it important. Sheep were brought by rail along the

Marches line and also from the Heart of Wales route, running through Central Wales. The junction station was known as Craven Arms and Stokesay, reflecting the importance of the castle. Today, it is simply called Craven Arms. The quiet town offers a pleasant respite on the route.

Acton Scott working farm

REFRESHMENT

There is a cafe at Acton Scott Historic Working farm for those who are visiting. Otherwise, the only place of refreshment is Craven Arms.

ACCOMMODATION

There is accommodation at Acton Scott, Strefford and Craven Arms.

PUBLIC TRANSPORT

The Marches railway line at Church Stretton and Craven Arms. Midland Red offer a Monday to Saturday service which calls at Marshbrook, a mile away from Acton Scott. Contact Shropshire Busline on (0345) 056785.

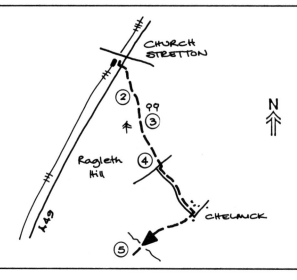

THE WALK

1. Leave Church Stretton railway station from the southbound platform (trains to Hereford and Cardiff). Cross the main A49 road with extreme caution and pass to the right of the Sandford Hotel into Clive Avenue to climb a bank and then turn left into Ragleth Road. A little way up this street turn right up Poplar Drive where the path is signposted to Chelmick.

2. At the end of the short street a path continues toward the wood and a Woodland Trust Walk is marked ahead. Do not be tempted but turn left instead to pass by the rear of a house and then right to cross a stile and climb steeply through the wood with wire fencing to your left. The path begins to move away from the fence and then curves left again. Avoid other paths leading off to the right and simply keep climbing until the route emerges onto moorland.

3. Cross the stile and make your way ahead to another stile and lane. Go down the lane to a road, turn right and then next left along the road signposted to Chelmick, straight ahead and ignoring a lane soon off to the left signposted to Hope Bowdler.

4. The minor road winds its way down to Chelmick hamlet where the walker bears right at the sharp left corner by Chelmick farm which

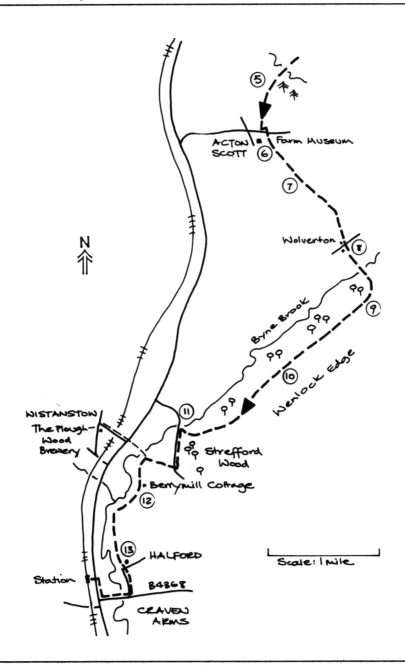

appears to make up the best part of the settlement. Almost immediately bear slightly right again along a bridleway through a gateway. The bridleway soon meets two gateways. Choose the one on the right and follow the hedge on the left as it descends towards Rag Batch. Go over the stile by a gate and descend to the brook. Avoid the gate on the left before the brook but keep ahead into a field where there is a junction of tracks. Bear left and go through a gate. The next section is not easy to follow but head slightly right across the field to the brow and then towards a spot approximately 30 metres from the far field corner. Look for a narrow path down to a footbridge across the Chelmick brook.

5. The path climbs away from the bridge along a slightly sunken track following the hedge on the left. It proceeds through a gate and keeps as close to the hedge on the left as is feasible. Continue ahead down to a ford and cross a stile by the second gate on the left. Follow the tractor track as it curves right to a gate leading onto a metalled road opposite Acton Scott farm. Bear left and, at the entrance to Acton Scott Farming Museum, go right to cross a stile leading to a picnic area.

6. Walk diagonally over the green to a stile and once over bear slightly right towards the far field corner. Cross another stile and dip into a wood. The path descends and then bends to the left to leave by way of another stile. Turn right and walk down the field to cross another stile. Cut the corner of the field to cross the next stile into a very large field, parkland but with a strong thistle growth.

7. Head very slightly right, the only marker being an old stile remaining from a grubbed hedge. Then proceed onwards in a similar direction over a sleeper bridge and moving closer to the tapering end of the pasture. Look for a stile to the left of a gate and cross into a patch of land dominated by scrub. Bear left, going over a bridge and one time track of the old railway route to Much Wenlock. Walk to a stile and into a large field. Head slightly right to the far right top corner where the path meets a track. Follow this to the outbuildings of Wolverton farm.

8. Cross the road and bear slightly left to walk by a silo and barn in a field. At the end of the buildings head very slightly right over the field to a footbridge. Once across, turn left and head slightly right to join a truncated hedgerow. Walk up the field on the left hand side of the hedge to a gap leading into the woodland. Do not be tempted to follow well

used paths leading right. Instead keep slightly left at first but shortly the path becomes clearer as it begins to curve right, moving away from the boundary hedge as it climbs the slope of Wenlock Edge. The climb continues beneath the ancient deciduous broadleaves until reaching the top at a junction of well worn tracks.

9. Turn right onto the first track running along the Edge. This continues for well over half a mile without any real view at all. Avoid paths leading off to the left towards open country and those dipping away steeply on the right. Your way is ahead along the Edge. It moves closer to the hedge on the left of the wood allowing limited views to Westhope and to Flounder's Folly on Callow Hill, a tower named after Benjamin Flounder. He paid for the work to be completed in 1838 possibly as a flamboyant boundary marker, although some have suggested that Mr Flounder had it built to keep locals in work. The path narrows and then widens, passes by outcrops of limestone and then leads into an opening.

10. Continue ahead along a path which has been opened to a track for forestry purposes. Shortly, look out for an opening on the right. This narrower path drops away here to the right and then curves left to a gate. It continues to descend more gently between hedgerows to a road. Bear left and left again at Strefford ford.

11. Pass by the forestry road on the left leading into Strefford wood. The metalled road then dips and it is here that you look for a stile and footbridge on the right. Once over, keep ahead through a field, near to the stream on the right, a tributary of the Quinny brook. Cross a stile into the next field and proceed ahead once again almost to the brook but beforehand turn left to cross a stile. Go straight ahead to a gateway and follow a track towards Berrymill cottage.

12. Go over the drive and walk ahead between huts and fencing along a track to a stile and into a pasture. Continue ahead through a narrow green field between woodland and the now much wider Quinny Brook just above its confluence with the River Onny. Head for a stile beneath the trees. This leads into thick woodland where the walker should be watchful for the remnants of a former collapsed iron fence. The path soon exits by way of two stiles in succession and continues straight on to the left of a line of knarled hawthorns. Go through the gate and walk

ahead to cross a stile by another gate. Bear slightly right to walk down a lane which, within paces, joins a road.

13. Bear left and follow this past the hamlet of Halford, not much more than a collection of farms, some of which have converted outbuildings into dwellings in a sympathetic manner.

At the junction turn right into Craven Arms for refreshment or accommodation. Those seeking the railway station should turn right at the main road and in a short distance turn left as signposted.

14. Those continuing can take a shorter route to Stokesay castle, by-passing the town if required. On the road approaching Craven Arms,

cross the road and a stile before the bridge over the Onny river. The path follows the river bank at first but then cuts across the field to a white foot-bridge. Cross this and pass between houses onto a road then keep ahead through an old quarter of town along a drive which soon leads to a stile. Cross this and walk ahead to another stile exiting onto the busy A49 road. Cross the road and join the pavement, where a left turn is made.

Stokesay Castle

CRAVEN ARMS TO LUDLOW

START: Craven Arms Railway Station

DISTANCE: 20 km (13 mls)

MAPS: Pathfinder Sheets 931 Craven Arms and 951 Ludlow

ROUTE DESCRIPTION

Passing by Stokesay Castle, the route climbs away to the gentle hills to the west of the Onny Valley, truncated by deep sided valleys known as gutters or dingles. Marches Way takes the walker through Aldon Gutter and near to the Wernlas Rare Breeds Collection before following more gentle terrain to Bromfield and through parkland to Ludlow.

FEATURES

Stokesay Castle

It is all the guide books say it is, a splendid fortified manor house, built of stone and with an equally fascinating half-timbered gatehouse. Built as a fortress initially, then altered through the centuries to make it a more comfortable dwelling, Stokesay was unbelievably abandoned in the 1720s and used as a barn. It was only through the endeavours of the Allcroft family in the mid nineteenth century, who devoted their lives to restore this property that it exists today.

Wernlas Collection, Brandhill

The Shropshire Centre of rare breeds displays a variety of old farm animal breeds with names such as Rhode Island Red and Leghorns. Those with a soft spot for pigs will not be disappointed nor will you be able to count the range of hens and cockerels strutting about the place. The Collection is open daily except Mondays from mid March to early November and to a lesser extent during the winter.

Bromfield

The crumbling, half timbered gatehouse on the road from Marches Way to the village centre was once an entrance to a priory, with the church being the remnants of an earlier and much larger building. The chancel ceiling, dating from the 17th century, caused a stir at the time for it is lacking in taste but is nevertheless of interest to the historian. The church contains many artefacts including a memorial to Henry Hickman who spent much of his life pioneering the use of anaesthetics.

Ludlow

Standing majestically above the Teme, Ludlow Castle and Ludlow church entices the walker into this handsome Marches town. Having gained wealth from trading wool, the town grew up as a fashionable domicile for wealthy townspeople. The range and style of buildings that they built have been preserved for us to see today. What is particularly impressive is they are still functioning as offices, shops and inns such as the famous half timbered Feathers Hotel in Corve Street. Ludlow is the resting place of poet A.E. Housman and a memorial tablet marking the burial place of his ashes can be found at Ludlow church. The sleepy nature of the area portrayed in his collection of poems "A Shropshire Lad" does not apply to Ludlow for its streets are packed with traffic.

The Feathers Hotel, Ludlow

REFRESHMENT

There is a cafe at Onibury old station house and **The Hollybush Inn** just around the corner is open from noon until 3 pm and then from 7 pm in the evening on Monday to Saturday. Usual opening times on Sundays. **The Hollybush** serves Ruddles and Websters draught beers and food. This is approximately half a mile from Whittytree.

The Clive Arms at Bromfield also serves refreshment. It is open from 11.30 a.m. until 2.30 p.m. and then again from 6.30 p.m. on Mondays to Saturdays, offering draught bass and usually a guest beer as well as food. The pub was once a farmhouse dating from Georgian times, but only being converted to a hostelry in 1977.

Ludlow has several cafes and inns.

ACCOMMODATION

At Onibury and Ludlow.

PUBLIC TRANSPORT

Midland Red serves Onibury and Bromfield on Monday to Saturday. Contact Shropshire Busline on (0345) 056785.

THE WALK

1. From Craven Arms railway station, leave by the access road to the main A49 road. Stay on this side of the road and walk through the town, unless diverting for toilets, the post office or refreshment. The road is busy and therefore not too healthy but it is a matter of ten minutes to walk out of town to Stokesay. A path leaves the main road on the right to join an access lane to Stokesay Castle.

2. Follow the lane to the entrance of the car park on one side and castle on the other. Your way is ahead to the left of the pool, which has been low in water for several years now, towards a farm. Before the buildings, bear right through a barred gate and walk along an access track to the railway line. Be warned, the trains move at considerable speed on this line so cross with care by way of the stiles. Pass by the house and walk

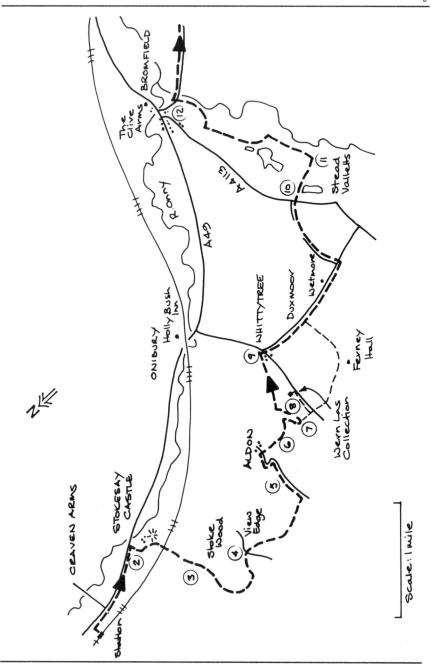

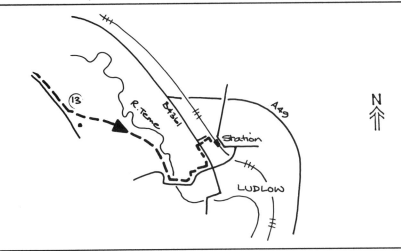

up the green lane to a gate. Head slightly right across the field, climbing very gently now to a stile. Cross this and walk in a similar direction towards another stile and then onward to Stoke wood. The old V stile cannot be seen at first but a well-worn path heads in the right direction.

3. Cross the stile into the wood and walk a few metres to join another path where the walker bears right. This leads along the edge of the wood until a stile is reached by a cottage known as Clapping Wicket. Cross the stile and walk up the drive for about fifty paces before turning left along a line that looks as if it would have been a hedge at one time. Do not go over the stile into the wood. Instead, bear right and walk along the field's edge to cross another stile. Then, join a track in the woodland but only for a short distance before re- emerging into a horseshoe-shaped field offering superb views across to Wales. Bear left up the field and begin to climb. Look for the waymark on the left directing the walker back into woodland and up what looks to be an old sunken lane. As the path climbs towards the summit of View Edge cross a stile and walk ahead by a garden to a tarmac road.

4. Bear left very briefly to pass by a pretty garden before going right over a stile opposite a barn. Bear slightly right, keeping company with the hedge on the right and cross a stile into the next field. Proceed ahead, bearing slightly left to another stile and then walk straight on with a hedge to your left. When approaching the far corner, go left through a gateway. At the bottom of the field proceed through another

gateway and follow the track to pass by a farm on the left and by a barn to the right. At the metalled road turn left to follow a particularly scenic section through to Whittytree.

5. Follow this road towards the hamlet of Aldon, a group of old farm buildings not much altered over the years. The road soon dips steeply into Springhead Gutter to cross a stream and then climbs equally ferociously up a bank. Towards the top look for a bridleway off to the right (signposted) and go through a bridle gate. Head right down a woodland path near to the wood's edge with a derelict cottage beneath in the valley. The path leads down to the valley floor, crossing a nettled patch to enter woodland again, the landmark being an old cottage ahead. The path leads slightly right and then left, passing old netting where pheasants have been bred previously.

6. The path crosses a stile to the right of a cottage, and leads across a track, continuing ahead through a wood known as The Larches. It curves around right into Brandhill Gutter and to a trickle of a stream. Cross it and bear left. Pass by an overgrown track on the right to a stile leading into a field. You might have noticed more than one derelict building in the gutter which somehow gives the place a feel of sadness, knowing that these dwellings are now lost forever.

7. Those wishing to visit the Wernlas Collection of Rare Breeds should climb up the bank diagonally to a stile and then proceed ahead along a corralled path to a road, known as Green Lane. Bear left to walk down to the entrance of the centre on the left.

There is an alternative route to join Marches Way from the centre. From Wernlas turn right to walk up the hill for a short distance. Turn left to cross a stile by a large gate and follow the field's edge to cross a stile in the next boundary. Walk down to a stile leading into Duxmoor Dingle. The path drops to a footbridge and then climbs, slightly left up the wooded bank to a stile.

Cross the road and a stile by a lodge to enter park land. Bear very slightly left to a stile just to the left of Ferney Hall. The path crosses a drive and bears slightly left through a gate into a field again. Follow the fence on the left down to a track, crossing fencing in two places. Cross the track and enter a small plantation. The path keeps to the left boundary and cuts across to a double stile. In the next field keep ahead with a hedge to your right to a stile by a gate. Turn right on the road to join Marches Way again as described in paragraph 8.

8. Those not visiting the Wernlas Collection should bear left once over the stile in Brandhill Dingle and walk along the valley edge rising to go through a gateway and then moving closer to the stream again. It continues to a stile and into woodland. The path continues ahead dipping towards the stream and then climbs slightly as it bears gently right through the woods. It continues ahead through a patch of dreaded rhododendrons (nice to look, at but a killer of other plants around it) to a gate. Follow the green track as it rises slowly away from the pools to climb along a hillside to a wall and barn. Go through a gate by the barn and ahead to another, then onto a road at Whittytree by a telephone kiosk. Those seeking a cut off point or refreshment in Onibury, should turn left for a half mile walk.

9. Otherwise, bear slightly right to take the left fork leading to Duxmoor and onto Wetmore farm on the left – about a mile of road walking. After Wetmore farm, take the next turning left along a narrow tarmac lane to a Wetmore cottage. The lane becomes a green track passing through a small scrub area and soon enters a main tractor track. Turn left to pass by Cookeridge cottages and continue ahead to the main A4113 road.

10. Cross this and bear slightly right and then left to pass by an old lodge known as Decoy cottage and a pool which is fished by a club bearing a similar name. Just beyond, as the track bears right towards Stead Vallets farm, go left through a gateway and bear right along this large field. The path keeps to the field edge, bearing left at the far corner and left again at the top right corner to reach, eventually, a gate in the next bottom corner.

11. Go right through it and follow the hedge on the left along the edge of another large field. This leads to a tractor bridge across a stream at the next field boundary. Once over bear right to follow the field's edge on the right to the banks of the Teme and to a stile onto a road at Bromfield by the bridge.

12. At Bromfield, pass by the church and old gateway if you seek a shop, The Clive Arms or a bus. Otherwise bear right to go over the bridge.

Follow the road to the right of the lodge house, passing through parkland. Ignore the fork to the right but continue ahead until the road narrows and descends, through a gateway, over a stream and then rises by a house.

13. Before the farm, go left through a gate as signposted. This green track leads to a field where the walker bears slightly right, with Ludlow church seen on the horizon. The path leads down to a stile and footbridge over a small stream. Keep ahead to the trees and then bear right along the field boundary to cross a stile and then ahead once again to cross another stile. The path then veers to the left to cross a footbridge and a stile situated in wet ground. It then climbs up a bank and continues ahead for a short distance before bearing slightly right in the direction of the Cliff Arms hotel and caravan site. Cross a stile onto the road and bear left for Ludlow.

14. The road joins another and continues ahead over Dinham Bridge and climbs a bank. Bear left half way up along a road known as Dinham up to the castle and then turn right into Market Square. Continue ahead by the old Butter Market and into King Street. Bear left into Corve Street to pass the famous Feathers Hotel and down to Station Street on the right which leads by the cattle market to the railway station.

LUDLOW TO YARPOLE

START: Ludlow Railway Station

DISTANCE: 18 km (11 mls)

MAPS: Pathfinder Sheets 951 Ludlow and 972 Tenbury Wells and Mortimer's Cross.

ROUTE DESCRIPTION

Marches Way rises through the woodlands of Mortimer's Forest and High Vinnals to Hanway, Orleton and Bircher Commons, very out of the way places. Progress through the ancient lands of Croft Ambrey to the fish pools of Croft Castle and then to the delightful village of Yarpole. This is an exceedingly good stretch of the route through tucked away border countryside.

FEATURES

Croft Ambrey hillfort

The ancient earth ramparts of this Iron Age hillfort can be seen higher up the ridge from Marches Way. Detailed excavations have revealed that this was an important settlement in prehistoric times.

Croft Castle

This fifteenth century stone house (with later additions) and church are now in the hands of the National Trust, although still occupied by the Croft family. The church contains many memorials to the family who have lived here for the best part of the past nine centuries. The formal gardens are also open to the public.

Yarpole

This out-of-the-way village nestles around the ancient church, much restored throughout the centuries but with a detached tower, one of six in Herefordshire. There are many interesting buildings in the village –

including The Bakehouse, once a medieval gateway, standing on the other side of the stream. The manor has long since gone.

REFRESHMENT

There is a shop-cum-cafe in Yarpole and **The Bell Inn**, a sixteenth century inn which had its own working mill and cider press until recent years. It now sells Bulmers draught cider and a tasty pint of Wood from Shropshire. The Bell is open from 1130 until 2.30 pm on Monday to Saturday, reopening again at 6.30 pm. Usual Sunday hours. Food served throughout the week.

The Bell Inn

ACCOMMODATION

There is accommodation available in the Yarpole and Luston area, two miles away.

PUBLIC TRANSPORT

There is one cut-off point at Hanway Common where walkers can divert to Richards Castle, where Midland Red operate a Monday to Saturday service to Ludlow and Leominster. Phone (0345) 212555.

Yarpole Church

THE WALK

1. Leave Ludlow railway station entrance and turn right along Station Drive, then turning left into Corve street to pass by several half timbered premises, including The Feathers Hotel. At the top of the road turn right into King Street, pass by the Butter Cross and into the Market Place leading to the castle entrance. Turn left before the castle to descend by Dinham House along a road known as Dinham. The road joins another, leading down to Dinham Bridge. Go over and follow the road around to the next corner where Marches Way enters Ludlow.

2. However, on this outward journey walk up the steep climb to the next sharp bend. Here, go ahead along the second track on the right, as signposted. Within a few paces, bear left up a narrow but well-walked woodland footpath to re-emerge onto the road higher up by a house. Bear left for 10 metres and then go right at the turning and signpost for Northwood farm.

3. Turn right onto the farm drive but as this forks left almost immediately, walk straight on up a track towards the wood and then bear left within a few paces into woodland. The path keeps company

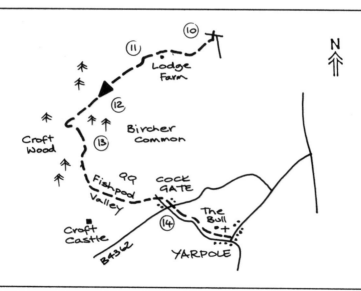

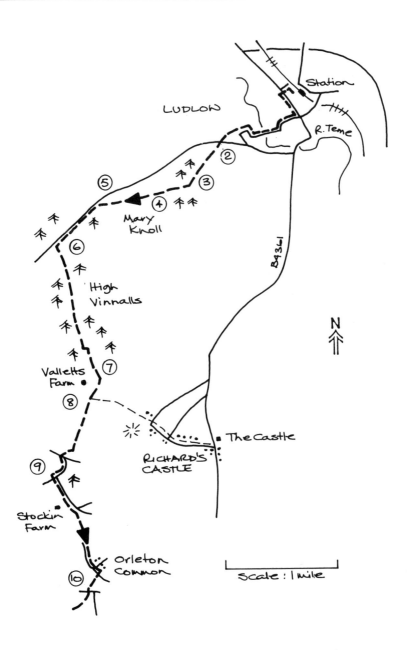

with the boundary hedge on the left and is well worn. It is also used by horse riders so can get a little muddy at times. It climbs up to an opening, where the path continues up to the field boundary before turning right and then very shortly left at the next junction. The path continues to rise with the boundary to the left and then comes to a junction of paths where there's a seat and information board just ahead.

4. Go right along a slightly sunken track (or the adjacent woodland path marked with yellow waymarks) which soon narrows and then cross a main forestry track at Point 5 on the forest markers. Keep ahead to meet another forestry track. Bear right here and the track curves around to the left to meet another main track coming in from the right. Keep ahead along this to exit eventually from the wood at a barred gate.

5. The path passes to the left of a barn and then along the hedge curving to the right and to exit by a gate at a road at Mary Knoll. Turn left and walk along the road, rising at first to Hazel Coppice then continue down the hill to High Vinnals picnic site and car park.

6. Turn left to follow the main track which passes to the right of the parking and picnic area. Be vigilant on this section for the forest tracks look very similar. Walk up to an elongated triangular junction and then bear left but be sure to turn first right almost immediately. (There is an alternative second right turning which leads onto the higher ground of High Vinnals). The lower route, however still offers excellent views across to Juniper hill and Aston as it climbs to meet another track coming in from the left and then a main track. Bear left here for another steep climb up to a left hand corner. The right of way is shown to the right here. Before reaching a hedge, turn left up a narrower path beneath trees to join a main green path, where you turn right. Alternatively, some locals simply follow the main forestry track left at the corner mentioned above and at the crossroads go right along the wide green path mentioned above.

7. This gives out shortly at a gate onto the upper reaches of Hanway Common. The path follows the hedge to the right as it curves gently around to the right to cross an access road leading up to Valletts farm.

Those wishing to divert to Richards Castle should bear left down this road which leads to the church and castle, which can be seen below.

There is a short walk down a quiet lane from the church to The Castle Inn on the B4361 where buses return to Hereford, Leominster and Ludlow.

8. Otherwise, head very slightly left across the field towards a far and tapering corner to go through a gateway and into a green lane. This is wide at first but narrows and drops down to a road by cottages at a place known as The Goggin which sounds and looks as if it could well be out of The Hobbit.

9. Turn left and at the next junction bear right up a steep hill to another road junction just over the summit. Turn left here and follow this through woodland with Stockin farm on the right below. Bear right just before the next road junction down a bridleway towards a stream and to a gateway. This passes by a house and up to a lane where the walker bears left through the hamlet of Orleton Common, a peaceful Hereford-shire backwater.

9. Pass by the chapel which stands on the other side of the stream running alongside the road. At the next road junction bear right. Very shortly, look for a road bearing right by a house. This passes another large house and outbuildings but be sure to keep ahead along a short and narrow link path up to the Ashley Moor road once again. Turn right and the road curves sharply left to pass two houses. After the second, bear right through a gate and follow the hedge on the right up the field, this section of route offering splendid views over North Herefordshire.

10. This was at once an old cart track, and the line of the route and gateways still remain. Go through another two gates ahead and then follow the winding track up to the ancient farmhouse, Lodge farm. Pass to the right of the house and buildings, through to another gate and then keep ahead with the hedge to your right. The track climbs a bracken clad bank to another gateway and up to the top corner of this valley edge field. Here, the path bears left to another gate which leads onto Bircher Common.

11. Bear slightly right on this wide green expanse of common. The path parallels the hedge on the right up to the far top corner, with a mass of coniferous woodland bordering it. Go over the stile into Croft Wood, rather than the wicket gate to the right. At the first junction keep right

and then proceed through the mainly coniferous woodland, avoiding the temptation to bear left along this section. In about half a mile, where a wide green path comes in from the right and as the main track begins to curve more sharply left, look for a narrow path off to the left, sometimes overgrown in summer.

12. This leads down to another forestry track. Bear left here on this loop and as it curves right look for a narrow path on the right. The path, once again sometimes overgrown, leaves this main track to duck into the gully below and descends it to another track where a post displays several markers.

13. Turn right here and follow the main track down into Fishpool valley. Pass the first fishpond and take the lower fork and again at the next fork, the pools always being almost immediately to your left. The track, however, soon begins to climb gently up to the drive to Croft Castle. Turn left along it to the lodge house and then bear right to cross the main B4362 at Cock Gate.

14. The lane passes the village hall and then descends into Yarpole village to the Bell public house, the church and shop-cum-bakery. At the junction by the latter turn right.

YARPOLE TO LEOMINSTER

START: Yarpole Church

DISTANCE: 10 km (6 mls)

MAPS: Pathfinder Sheets 992 Tenbury Wells and Mortimer's Cross, and 994 Leominster

ROUTE DESCRIPTION

This gentler section follows footpaths through meadows to Eye Manor and church then onwards along Moreton Ride to skirt the parkland of Berrington Hall. The path then joins the old Kington and Leominster canal before traversing fields to Leominster town.

FEATURES

Eye Manor

Eye Manor, built in 1680, is famous for its Renaissance ceilings. It is unfortunately not open to the public. Next to it stands the appealing little church of Eye.

Black and White

The Marches is known for its "Black and White" villages and homesteads. The term refers to the building of timbered and half-timbered houses and barns in this area. Some of the properties date from medieval times when wattle and daub was interlaced between oak timbers. Most, however, are from later times and the Victorians moved towards the more ornate timber and brick construction with a whitewash finish.

Berrington Hall

Managed by the National Trust, Berrington Hall was built in the 1780s for Thomas Harley. The surrounding parklands were laid out by that well known landscape gardener, Capability Brown.

Leominster

Leominster, like Ludlow, grew in prosperity through

the sale of wool, known as "Lemster Ore" locally. A place of religious significance, Leominster priory survives as a monument to earlier monastic settlements. Not that it has always been peaceful here. The town suffered siege and plunder throughout the middle ages. It still retains a strong agricultural base and much of the fine half-timbered and Georgian architecture can be seen by walking along its narrow thoroughfares.

REFRESHMENT

There are several cafes and public houses in Leominster. At the time of writing, The Balance Inn in Luston had closed but who knows it may enjoy a new lease of life again.

ACCOMMODATION

Luston and Leominster

PUBLIC TRANSPORT

Midland Red run between Leominster and Ludlow to Luston. Phone (0345) 212555.

Leominster has a daily service on the Marches Railway line.

THE WALK

1. From the entrance gate to Yarpole church turn left to walk to a junction. Go right and the road bends left and then right as it leaves the village. Look for a stile on the left which leads into a field and across to another stile a little way to the left of a gateway. The path curves gently right in the next field to a small bridge across the stream. Go over it and bear slightly right for a stile in the hedge opposite. Cross this and head slightly right across a large field to a gate half-way across.

2. Go through the gateway and bear slightly right to the far right corner with Lady Meadow farm to the left. Go through a gate and head very slightly left across the field to a stile which exits onto a main road.

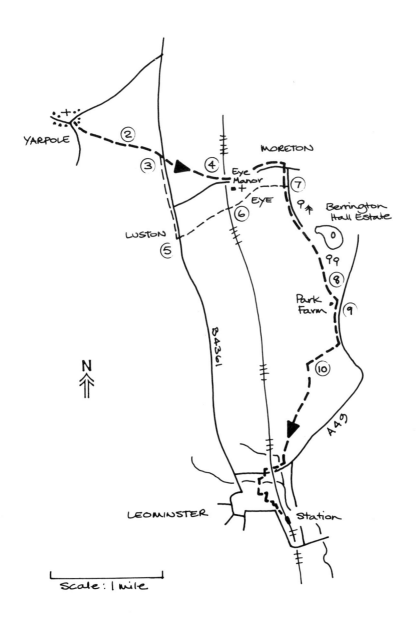

3. Those by-passing Luston should cross the B4361 and a stile opposite to the left of a lodge. Keep ahead along the hedge on the right and go through a gate into the next field. Once again,' follow the hedge on the right ahead to a gate which brings the walker to a drive by a house on the left and then one on the right. Keep ahead to cross a stile into the next field and then bear slightly left towards a village hall. Walk along the fence ahead to cross a stile onto a road known as Eye lane.

4. Bear left and follow the lane past Court Farm and Eye Manor and church on the right. The road continues up to the hamlet of Moreton where the walker bears right onto a bridleway to pass by Moreton farm.

5. Those joining or diverting at Luston should follow the route outlined in this paragraph and paragraph 6. The walk across fields to Eye begins at an unobtrusive gated green track leading off from a point opposite Luston Methodist chapel. This passes between gardens to a pasture. Keep ahead to a stile and once across proceed slightly left over a field and through a gateway before heading slightly left again to cross two stiles guarding a footbridge. Keep ahead again to the railway and cross with extreme caution.

6. Keep ahead, once again, to cross a concrete track by way of gates and then bear slightly left towards a hedge, unless visiting Eye church (by going over the stile on the left) keep ahead to a gate. This brings the walker into a large field where the path is very slightly left to a stile and footbridge over the channel known as Main Ditch. In the next field bear left to the field corner and then right to keep ahead, crossing the scant remains of the Leominster Canal to a gateway leading to a bridleway, Moreton Ride.

7. The path joins a bridleway here and all walkers should be re-united again on this section alongside Berrington Hall estate, the work of Henry Holland in the latter part of the eighteenth century. Go right along this track which soon leads to a field's edge then into a wood, through two wicket gates and over a footbridge in wet ground with the keeper's lodge to the left. As the old fence bears left you bear slightly right to cross a stile adjacent to a gate walking in the direction of Park farm.

8. Before the track goes through the next gateway closer to the farm head slightly left up through a gateway and in the direction of two large oaks

and the main A49 road. The bridleway exits through a gate and up a steep embankment to the roadside.

9. The next five minutes of road walking is hardly pleasant but the verge is wide. Turn right and walk beyond the lay-by, often frequented by lorry drivers stopping for refreshment at a mobile cafe. Turn right down the next track towards Moors farm, as signposted off the road. Within a very short distance cross a stile on the left leading into a field and then follow the green track along the side of the gently curving dip of the Kington, Leominster and Stourport canal to another stile. Cross this and walk along the field's edge to a barred gate just beyond a barn.

10. Go through the gate and head slightly left across this large field to the far corner. Cross two bridges in succession and then go left to another stile. From this, go ahead to a bridge and through a gate. Cross another stile by a gate, go over the Ridgemoor Brook and then bear right before the service station forecourt along a green path to the main road. Cross the road, Mill Street, along the pavement to a point beyond the level crossing where a path leads off to the left by a cottage and opposite

Carvings, The Grange (Leominster District Council)

a half timbered house. This ancient by way leads to an iron bridge dating from 1844 which leads into a narrow lane up to Leominster Priory church and grounds. Turn right along Church street for the town centre. Those seeking the railway station should proceed ahead through the churchyard, with the priory to the left. Continue slightly left across the park to Pinsley Road, with the elegant Grange ahead. This road twists and winds its way to the corner of Etnam street. Keep ahead for a short distance to the railway station entrance on the left.

LEOMINSTER TO DINMORE .

START: Leominster Railway Station

DISTANCE: 16 km (10 mls)

MAPS: Pathfinder Sheet 994 Leominster

ROUTE DESCRIPTION

Once out of Leominster, the route meanders through the Arrow valley to Ivington and then along roads and tracks to the edge of Camp Wood, with hop yards below, the residue of a one-time widespread hop growing business in this part of the county. From here, the path passes through orchards and Gattertop farm to Upper Hill. It then climbs Winsley Hill and onto Dinmore, with superb views across Herefordshire to The Malvern hills.

FEATURES

Upper Hill

The quiet hamlet of Upper Hill had a pub known as The Spitfire (formerly The Red Lion) and named after a spitfire plane which used to stand in front of it. The pub and plane have now gone but there is still a Swift jet fighter, dating from the early 1950s, on the forecourt of a warehouse here.

Queenswood Country Park, Dinmore Hill

The country park and arboretum have been developed in recent years with the reconstruction of the old Essex Arms from Hereford as a Visitor Centre, shop and cafe.

REFRESHMENT

There is a cafe at Queenswood, Dinmore Hill

Cider

The local beverage in days gone by in these parts would have been cider rather than ale. The production of cider and perry grew from a farmhouse pre-occupation to a world-wide business with the rise of Bulmers Cider in the past one hundred years. The unfortunate point is that much of the cider made is pasteurised, chilled and made fizzy, hence losing its distinctive qualities and taste.

In Herefordshire, there has been something of a revival of local, small scale cider producers and champions of this have been Ivor and Susie Dunkerton, who make delicious cider and perry at Luntley in Herefordshire. They comment: "It is a great joy to us to be offered by a farmer an ancient cider apple variety, to press it for the very first time, to smell its unique aroma and taste the darkening juice, to ferment it and re-discover an excellent cider".

They have also been instrumental in saving old varieties of cider and perry pear trees as the traditional orchard so that specialist natural beverages can be produced for generations to come.

Dunkerton's Cider

ACCOMMODATION

Newtown between Leominster and Ivington.

PUBLIC TRANSPORT

Primrose Motors operate a bus service on Monday to Saturday between Leominster and Upper Hill. Telephone (0568) 612271 for details.

Midland Red West run to Dinmore Hill daily. Contact (0345) 212 555.

THE WALK

1. From Leominster railway station, turn right and pass by a bus garage and public house on the right as the road bears left into Etnam Street. At the top bear left and at the next junction keep ahead at the roundabout along the old Hereford Road out of town, this also being a section of The Black and White Trail.

2. Look for a turning on the left into Leominster's main industrial estate and just beyond is a cemetery with chapel. Almost opposite this go right up a back road, known as Passa Lane. The road curves to pass by a house and then comes to a point where tracks bear left and right. Go left here and walk down to a barred gate. The path is signposted to the right to follow the field boundary to a stile in the opposite fence.

3. Cross the stile and small footbridge, with the River Arrow to the left. Walk along the field's edge for no more than twenty paces before striking ahead, rather than along the river bank, over the brow of the hill in this large field, keeping to the left of the isolated trees silhouetted on the landscape. Keep ahead to cross a footbridge which stands to the left of a group of trees and once over go straight ahead again in the direction of a modern red brick house.

4. The path meets a barred gate and enters a pleasant enough track on the right which leads up to a road at the hamlet of Newtown. Turn left and follow the road by the houses. Bear left (avoiding a turning to the right) across the flood plain of the Arrow to the hamlet of Ivington, first to pass an old mill on the right, then the very old farm of Ivingtonbury on the left. The Black and White trail exits right here. Your way is ahead, and around by the village church, school and bus shelter.

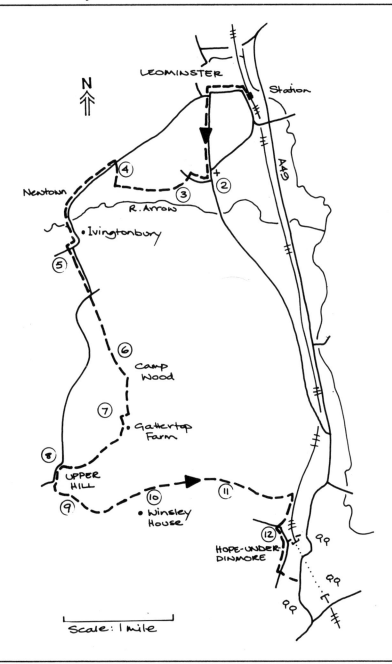

Scale: 1 mile

5. Bear left at the road junction, heading in the direction of Upper Hill as signposted. Just when the road begins to become a little tedious a junction appears. Cross directly over to walk down a farm access lane and pass by Park farm to walk a short section of green lane. This gives out into a field. Keep company with the hedge on your right as the track peters out and begins to climb to a gap in the next field boundary. This section is the subject of a proposed diversion. The path should, however, cut left across the field to a gate.

6. Once on the road bear left up to the edge of Camp wood, hiding the ramparts of Ivington Camp, a prehistoric hillfort. The road continues to climb and as it bears left, cross a stile on the right. Bear diagonally left to descend to the far bottom field corner to cross another stile. Once again, walkers might find a diversion here and be encouraged to simply walk ahead through the field from the bridle gate. The church spire which can be seen in the distance is at Weobley, one of the villages on The Black and White Trail. Continue ahead alongside the hedge on your right and go through a gateway on the right to walk alongside another hedge on the right, separating orchards, to a gate leading onto a road by a cottage.

The Marches Tour arriving at Weobley

7. This section is also the subject of diversion. The existing right of way is as described below but walkers might find a waymarked permissive path ahead, avoiding the farm and will find this easier. Otherwise, go left and walk towards the fine looking Gattertop farm. Approach the farmyard. The route on the Pathfinder map is towards the farm house and then right. Some local walkers, however, bear right along a farm track and then left to skirt the farm buildings. Just beyond the last building on the right bear right along a level track (rather than the one leading down the dip) away from the farm. This comes to two gates. Choose the one on the right and keep ahead with a hedge to your left. This leads to a small gate. Proceed through it and go straight on with a hedge on the right. Again, come to two gates. Choose the one on the right leading into a lane. This brings the walker to another track and bear right by the memorial down to a road in Upper Hill.

8. Turn left and walk along by houses as the road swings left at first then right to a junction. Turn left to pass a bus shelter and then an old chapel on the left by Swing Gate nursery. Go straight on to a junction and follow the road which curves left, still climbing to another junction, with a cottage to the left and a farm on the right.

Continue ahead across the green but be vigilant to look for a narrow green track leading off slightly left at a lower level. This is your way, down to a sleeper bridge and towards a half timbered cottage.

9. Bear right before the cottage to go through a gate into a field. Your way is ahead to a gateway and then to walk up a small field to cross a stile and ahead once again up the field to cross another stile on the side of the bank. Once over go left and shortly cross yet another stile. Head slightly right, climbing very gently now, to a stile in a fence. Cross this and proceed to another in the next field boundary. Go very slightly right across a pasture to cross a stile and the tops of the ancient Winsley House are just visible to the right.

10. Go ahead, not through a barred gate, but keeping the hedge to the left at first. Half way along bear slightly right to meet a stile which stands about 100 metres to the right of gate. Cross it and progress very slightly right heading just to the right of a decaying barn. The way is down hill now, more or less ahead through a succession of stiles, very often adjacent to gates in field boundaries. The views of Dinmore and to

the Malvern hills beyond are extensive and make this section a delight to walk.

11. Pass by a barn, cross an old stile by a barred gate and continue along a tractor track which begins to curve to the right as it descends Winsley Bank. However, leave the track to bear slightly left, heading for a stile by wooden fencing. Cross it and walk down the hill with a fence and hedge to the left, with views of Hope under Dinmore village beneath. The path joins another just before the Marches railway line. Bear right here and follow the railway embankment at first but then moving away from it, slightly right, and then heading to the right of the sturdy looking Block Cottages. Go through a gate and bear left down the track to go through another and slightly right down to a road.

12. Turn left and pass by houses down to a road junction. Go right over a stile here and then bear left to walk up the hillside to cross another stile on the left to a road once again. Bear right and walk up the hill between houses and cottages set back from the roadside. At a road junction, with an old cottage to the right, look for a stile and path on the left leading into Queenswood Country Park.

This climbs to cross a bridleway then continues ahead and upwards. Cross another track and keep ahead, the noise of the main A49 road becoming louder, to a commemorative stone. Those stopping awhile should bear right to the visitor centre.

13. Otherwise, cross the main road with extreme care for this is a dangerous spot. The cars simply travel too fast for comfort. Your way is signposted through woodland as a bridleway.

DINMORE TO HEREFORD

START: Queenswood Visitor centre

DISTANCE: 17 km (11 mls)

MAPS: Pathfinder sheets 994 Leominster and 1017 Hereford North

ROUTE DESCRIPTION

From Queenswood, the route descends to the Lugg valley at Bodenham and for the most part follows paths across fields to the villages of Marden, Sutton Saint Nicholas and Lyde before entering Hereford, ironically, through its industrial quarter.

FEATURES

Bodenham

Two miles away from Marches Way is Broadfield Court which has in recent years developed a well-respected vineyard. Winetasting tours are arranged. Bodenham church stands in an old part of Bodenham village next to the green running waters of the River Lugg. It dates from the fourteenth century but has been much restored during the last century.

Sutton Saint Nicholas

The Iron Age hillfort is easy to see, and Marches Way dissects it en route to the few houses which make up Sutton Saint Michael. King Ethelbert is said to have resided here for a time and was slain within the very walls. The village of Sutton Saint Nicholas has several charming houses set back from the crossroads.

Hereford

The city of Hereford, with its magnificent cathedral which houses the Mappa Mundi, is a busy centre. Its pedestrianised core is pleasant, as are the walks around the old castle grounds and cathedral precincts. There are several museums including a Cider Museum near Bulmers Cider, just off the Whitecross Road. The museum still brews its own cider and distils a special brandy to compete with the French. It is named after King Offa of Mercia. The Butter Market in High Town and the Cattle Market are reminders that Hereford is a market place for the borderlands.

'The Old House', Hereford (Hereford City Council)

REFRESHMENT

Marches Way passes **The Volunteer** at Marden, a lively village pub (street circus events, summertime fun events) open every day at noon through to 2.30 pm extended to 3pm on Friday to Sunday and in the evening from 7 pm onwards. The pub specialises in healthy lunch time snacks and has a paddock in the back for camping.

The Golden Cross at Sutton Saint Nicholas is a short diversion from the route, serving Banks bitter on handpump in the bar, is open from 11 am until 2.30 pm (4pm on Saturday) during the week and from between 6 pm and 6.30 pm at the start of the evening session. This friendly local welcomes ramblers.

ACCOMMODATION

Accommodation is available at Bodenham and Marden as well as Hereford.

PUBLIC TRANSPORT

A local bus service from Leominster to Hereford serves Bodenham, Marden and Sutton Saint Nicholas on Mondays to Saturdays. Telephone Lugg Valley Motors on (0568) 612759.

THE WALK

1. Cross the road by the commemorative stone as signposted and once over proceed through a gate into woodland known as Church Coppice, lying as it does above Hope-under-Dinmore church. The route leads to another main track. Bear right along this track which heads slightly left among tall trees. Keep ahead and the track leads into open countryside. At the junction keep ahead with a farm known as Henhouse in view.

2. The track passes to the right of the buildings, and through a barred gate. Just beyond a circular tree plantation of young trees, bear slightly right as waymarked and across a field to woodland with a view over to Bodenham church below. The path descends to a stile and to a wooded bank. It then descends more sharply to a stile and cross track. Bear left here and then almost immediately right to fall once again almost to the

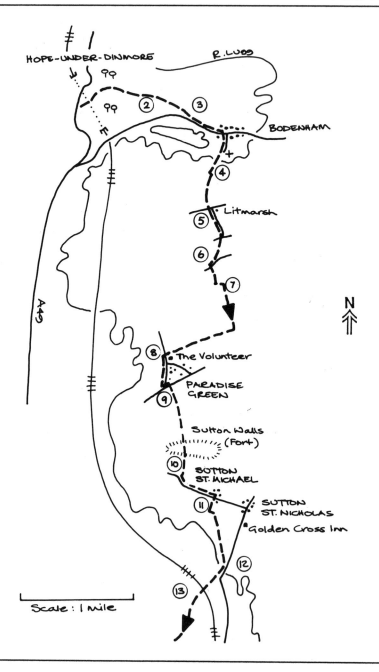

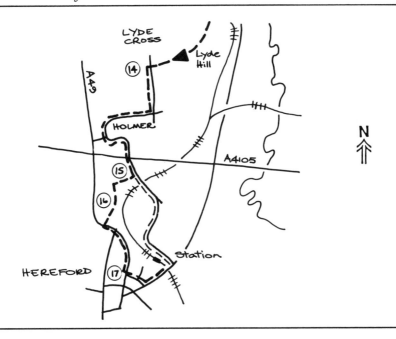

entrance of Bodenham Manor restaurant.

3. Turn left to walk along the road into Bodenham village and at the memorial, bear right along a road which winds down by the school and church. There is a little link path off to the right which also cuts through to the church if the walker wishes. Go through the lych-gate and walk to the right of the church and through the churchyard to a bridge across the river Lugg.

4. Cross a large meadow on a path signposted to Litmarsh in the direction of the Ashgrove wood. Cross a footbridge into the wood and climb up steps to a stile. Cross it and keep ahead, down the hillside towards a pool. Before it, turn left as waymarked to walk along a green swathe not far from the banks of the pool and cross a stile which leads to a track. Turn right and follow it through a gap and then it bears left to meet a road. Turn right here and then very shortly first left.

5. Walk by a few houses at Litmarsh and, at a sharp left corner with a turning to the right at Monmarsh, look for a stile on the right leading into a field. Cross it and continue slightly right through the field as

signposted, with Vauld farm standing on the left with a fine oast house in view.

Cross a stile in the top right hand corner and keep ahead to another stile by a signpost.

6.This exits onto a lane where the walker turns right. Just around the corner and before a tall hedge go left over a stile. Walk up the bank, bearing slightly left to cross a stile and then walk ahead to the far left corner where there is a stile in a thick-set hedge leading onto a bridle path. Go left and at the next junction bear right.

7. Follow this towards Hawkersland Cross. However, before reaching the houses, a parallel track comes alongside the bridleway. This also happens to be a right of way.

As the houses are approached, bear right through a gap to join and then cross the track and a stile – which has, in the past, been removed! Proceed almost ahead across the field to cross another stile. Keep ahead with a hedge to the left to another stile. Go over this and walk straight on again to the next corner and cross a stile. The path curves around a pond and then proceeds ahead to cross stiles guarding a footbridge. In the next paddock, walk straight on, keeping company with a hedge on the right. Go over a stile by a gate and walk ahead to a gateway. Go through it to pass between a cottage and house to exit onto a road. Turn left to pass by the Volunteer public house.

8. Your way from the pub is to keep ahead, passing by the old Blacksmiths and then turn left at the next main junction in Paradise Green. Then look for a path after the fourth bungalow on the right. The path is signposted along a little green way between gardens.

9. Cross a stream and go through a barred gate to walk up the field with the hedge to the left. Look for a gap shortly on the left and go through it. Bear right and go through a gap in the hedge, still proceeding ahead with a hedge to the right. Cross a stile on the right now bearing left to keep company with the hedge on the left. Cross another stile and then ahead again to cross a final stile leading into the wooded ramparts of Sutton walls. There is a good view of Marden church from here and also to the mysterious knolls at Canon and Kings Pyon.

10. The path climbs up to a track and walkers would be amazed to know that this area was once a site for tipping rubbish, hence the concrete road and remains of fencing. This leads by a house and to a road at Sutton Saint Michael. Cross the road and bear left to walk facing the traffic along a moderately busy road into Sutton Saint Nicholas. Pass by the chapel and at a minor crossroads (with a bridleway signposted on the left), turn right along a lane, signposted as a footpath, through a residential area to fields. Those seeking refreshment should, however, proceed ahead along the road to The Golden Cross public house.

11. Go through a barred gate by a pond and bear left following the water ditch until the path comes alongside the River Lugg. Look for a stile in the far corner of the narrow enclosure under a canopy of bushes. Walk ahead to cross two stiles in succession as the river meanders peacefully nearby. Walk straight ahead along the river bank to cross another stile and onto a gap in the next field boundary. Go through another field to cross a stile and onto a road.

12. Turn right and go over the bridge. Just beyond the corner proceed a few steps more to a stile on the right. Cross this and bear slightly left towards the top left corner of the field. Cross a stile on the left and then go over a footbridge on the right, before walking across a narrow strip of land to the railway, which must be crossed with care.

13. Go over a footbridge and stile, then walk up the field's edge to the corner where you cross a stile. The path enters a small pocket of woodland only to exit by way of a stile into a field. Here, the path runs alongside a hedge on the right, still climbing the slopes of Lyde Hill. There are views over to Hereford from here; for those feeling a little weary, it is only two miles now to this next port of call. Come to a gap and continue ahead again keeping company with a hedge on the right. This gives out at a gate. Go through it and climb up the hill bearing slightly right up to a tree on a hillside. Cross a stile and follow the tree line up to cross another stile. The path now begins to drop down alongside a hedge on the left to a double stile and by a house to a road at Lyde Cross.

14. Turn left and follow this quiet lane left as it descends to Munstone. At the next crossroads, bear right for the Rose Cottage Garden public house which has a lovely garden to be enjoyed on a fine summer's day.

The road leads down to the village of Holmer and at the next junction bear left into Attwood Lane. This continues by a golf range and small scale works to the Roman Road. Cross it and continue along Old School Lane. There are two options here. Those seeking a speedier but uneventful walk down to the railway station should go over the railway bridge and turn right into Kingsway. Walk through a residential estate to Barrs Court road which is followed, and then right and right again to the railway station as signposted at the traffic lights.

15. Otherwise, choose an alternative path as follows. Ironically, the most industrialised section of the route is in Hereford, a city known for its strong agrarian ties. Walk past the factory gates and then bear right along a narrow path corralled by tall fencing between two major works, known locally as Painters and Wiggins. The path turns left to cross a road by a security post and then between more works before bearing left to exit onto a road by offices.

16. Turn right to walk along Mortimer Street, then bear left on the main road to walk over the railway siding to Bulmer's cider factory. At the roundabout, keep ahead along Newtown Road. At the next mini roundabout, bear slightly right along Widemarsh Street to pass Coningsby Hospital on the left, now a museum. Those seeking the railway station should turn next left into Coningsby Street and at its far end continue through an old graveyard to Commercial Road. Bear left and walk up to the next set of traffic lights where the walker bears left again as signposted for the station.

17. Those continuing through Hereford should continue to walk along Widemarsh Street, crossing the inner ring road and into Hereford's shopping area. The road passes the pedestrianised High Town on the left. Turn left by Marks and Spencer and then first right along a pedestrian passage, crossing a road and onward along Church Street to the cathedral. Bear right in the cathedral precinct to join Broad Street and then ahead into KIng Street and left into Bridge Street.

HEREFORD TO ABBEYDORE

START: Hereford Railway Station

DISTANCE: 20 kms (13 mls)

MAPS: Pathfinder sheets 1040 Hereford (South) and 1039 Golden Valley.

ROUTE DESCRIPTION:

Marches Way leaves Hereford city along the banks of the Wye to continue through residential areas for over a mile before rising gently through farming country to villages of Clehonger and to Kingstone. From the latter the Way follows quiet paths into a very isolated agricultural community known as the Grey valley. There seems to be no satisfactory explanation of its name, given its beauty. Admittedly it seems not as lush as its neighbour, the Golden valley. Beyond the hamlet of Kerry's Gate, which is little more than a few houses and a telephone kiosk, the route descends to the River Dore, and to the ancient settlement of Abbeydore.

FEATURES:

Belmont Abbey

Dating from the nineteenth century, this intriguing piece of architecture is the work of Pugin, renowned for his skill in redesigning the House of Commons. The abbey is now the home to a public school. Some historians also suggest that Pugin had a hand in the restoration of nearby Clehonger Church which Marches Way also passes, the tell tale signs being the particularly ornate glasswork.

Kingstone

Described less than poetically in a "Shell Guide" in the 1950s as a slightly dull place, Kingstone nestles around a tidy little country church with parts dating back to the thirteenth century. Nearby stands the Bull

Ring public house, possibly once a bull bating site, not a dull pastime but nevertheless a disgusting one.

Abbey Dore Court Gardens

Marches Way passes this charming four acre garden which now includes a garden centre and a Teddy Bears Loft for those softies who still collect such endearing toys. There is also a restaurant open between 11 am and 5 pm when the gardens are open from late March to late October.

Abbey Dore

Surrounded by orchards which look as though they have been cultivated since the time of Adam and Eve, the solid red sandstone outline of this monastic enclave is a masterpiece of Early English architecture. Evidently saved by a local seventeenth century benefactor, Lord Scudamore, the abbey has been tended and conserved by subsequent generations. Originally built to house an order of Cistercian monks this abbey became a grand church for the local community.

Ewyas Harold

This village, larger than most for Herefordshire, stands mainly on the banks of the Dulas brook beneath the old motte and bailey castle and the church that almost certainly served the garrison nearby. The village pubs and shops are a testament to the way in which rural life need not be one of decline and loss of facilities.

REFRESHMENT:

The Vaga public house, Hunderton. This Hereford local has featured in the Good Beer Guide for years.

The Seven Stars, Clehonger. A well kept public house which offers a warm welcome, food and Whitbread beers to the traveller. Detour at Bowling Green farm by turning right down hill, cross over to bear left down Gosmore Road and then cross a stile on the right (opposite a cottage) to link through to the pub. It is open 1130 until 3 pm on Monday to Friday and a little later on Saturday afternoons, re-opening at 6.30 pm in the evenings. Sunday as usual. There are seats outside but children are not allowed in the bar.

The Bull Ring, Kingstone sells Whitbread beers.

The Neville Arms, Abbeydore. A very pleasant stop before climbing onto the common. There is always a good welcome, a choice of draught beers – Bass, Courage Best and Wadworth 6X, and food. The pub dates back to early times and the landlord and landlady say that there are so many yarns it could be the topic of an entire book! It is open 11 until 3 pm at lunch and from 7 pm in the evening. Usual Sunday opening.

ACCOMMODATION

Kingstone

PUBLIC TRANSPORT

Clehonger, Kingstone and Abbeydore are served by country buses. Contact Yeomans Canyon Travel on (0432) 356201 or Red and White on (06333) 5118.

THE WALK

1. From Hereford railway station entrance follow the station drive left, right and then left into Commercial Road. Turn right to walk past the Bus Station and cinema. At the top of the road, keep ahead at the major junction, i.e. by The Kerry Arms and along the pedestrianised Commercial Street into High Town. Before Marks and Spencer at the top left corner, go down a passage as indicated in paragraph 17 of the Dinmore to Hereford section.

2. The departure from the old Wye Bridge in Hereford is rather uneventful, following a riverside path beneath the litter strewn Greyfriars bridge, then along a stretch of river, with the earthworks of the one time Hereford to Abergavenny tram terminus on the left. The path passes beneath a fine looking old railway bridge and ahead to a narrow road in Hunderton. On the left is the Vaga public house in Vaga Street. Keep ahead, however and shortly the road curves left by flats in Goldenpost and at the next junction turn right down a track.

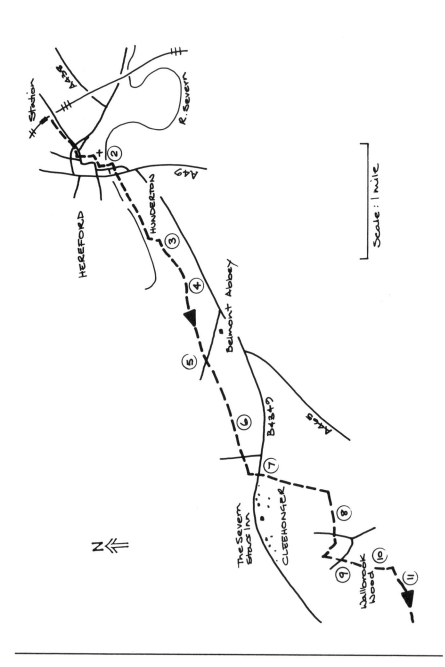

Scale : 1 mile

HEREFORD

Station

R. Severn

A438

A49

HUNDERTON

Belmont Abbey

B4349

A465

The Seven Stars Inn

CLEEHONGER

Wallbrook Wood

N

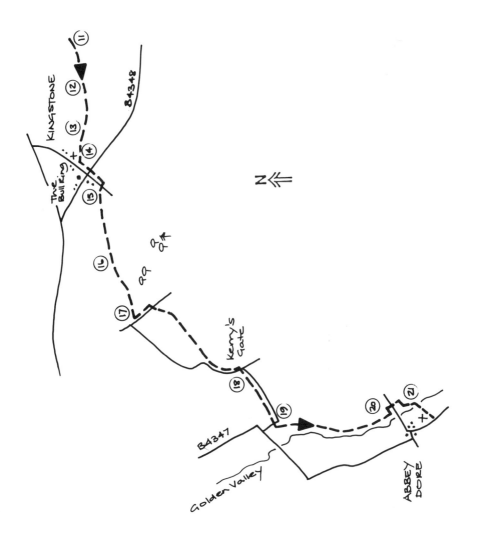

3. Cross a bridge and walk ahead along a path which was once in open countryside and is now surrounded by a modern housing estate. Cross the road and walk into Clehonger parish with a linear path making its way between houses alongside a stream. The clock tower of a well known supermarket stands for all to see on the left.

4. At the time of writing the following description is apt but the next two fields could be the scene of more building activity thus rendering the description into the realms of history. Keep to the path alongside the stream with part wall, part hedge to the right. At the top of this field the path leads through the hedge and heads slightly left to pass through old quarry workings. It then turns left and right to come alongside a hedge full of willow, alder and elder trees. There is a reasonable view of Hereford from here and Belmont Abbey ahead on the left. The path brings the walker to a stile in the top right field corner. Those wishing to visit the abbey can bear left before the stile and follow the hedge up to a stile leading onto a road. Turn right to re-join the route a little farther down the road on the left – as explained below in paragraph 5.

5. Cross it and walk a short section to another stile which exits onto a road to Ruckhall. Turn right to walk a few paces before crossing a stile on the left. Proceed along a hedge at first but then turn slightly right towards a stile in the hedge opposite. Cross this and enter a very large field, a classic example of hedges being grubbed in the interest of modern farming. Clehonger old village lies ahead, the landmark to aim for being the parish church. Head slightly right of the church, to the right of a large oak and by a delightful pond to a kissing gate and road.

6. Cross this and walk along a track which leads off to the right of the churchyard which gives out into a field behind the church. Keep company with the hedge on your right as the path rises to a stile and into the next field. Cross a stile by a gate and approach Bowling Green farm. Simply keep ahead and to the right of a large barn to a barred gate which exits onto a lane. Here you bear left to walk through the farm yard to the B4349 road.

7. Turn left, cross the road with great care and then bear right along a track, signposted, by a few houses and bungalows until the lane gives out into fields by way of a gate and across the field ahead. At the next field go through the gate ahead and onto a green track. At the next

junction bear right along another equally lovely track to exit onto a road by Mawfield farm.

8. Turn left and just after the corner go right through double barred gates into an orchard, with a view of the radar tracking station at nearby Madley airfield and the Merbach range and the Black Mountains beyond. Pass an old barn, go through a gateway and turn right. Keep alongside the hedge for the length of the orchard on the opposite side and then bear left down the field along what was until very recently a hedgerow. After 100 metres bear slightly right to walk towards a stile where paths meet. Do not cross the stile. Instead, turn around and soon bear slightly right towards the far bottom corner. There is a stile here, allowing the walker to exit onto the road.

9. Go over the road and through the barred gate. Head very slightly right and across a slope to a stile by a barred gate. Once over head in the same direction to a large hedge where a stile is crossed. Head slightly right across this next field to the far corner where the walker goes through a gate.

10. Bear left and head for the tapering far right corner of the next field, with Wallbrook wood to the right. The path crosses a stile in fencing and over a small bridge across a stream and then bears right towards the wood. After the gate it bears left and within a matter of paces turns right into Wallbrook wood. Keep slightly left through the wood, following waymarks, across a bridge and ahead again to a field.

11. Keep ahead to cross a stile in a low level and partly grubbed hedge. In the next field, go straight ahead to join a field corner which leads to a stile exiting onto the road.

12. Turn left for a few paces and then bear right through a double barred gate and walk directly down the field to a wood. Bear right at the edge and follow it around until it curves sharply left where a stile on the left leads into the covert.

The well worn path, muddy in places, brings the walker to a plank bridge across a small stream and to a stile. Once across, proceed through a narrow paddock to cross another bridge and stile. Then, head very slightly right to cross another awkward stile in a hedge, with a rural cottage to your right.

13. In this next field your way is slightly left towards Kingstone church. Cross a stile and follow a hedge with the farm on the left to enter the churchyard by way of a kissing gate.

14.Leave by the main gate to the left of the church onto a track which bears right down to the main road. Cross the junction and walk along the road to Cockyard to pass white bungalows on the right. Look for a ladder stile between a red brick cottage and bungalow on the right. The path follows the hedge on the left at first then cuts across slightly left to the far corner.

15. Go through the gate and head slightly right, crossing a prominent track, to a field corner which begins to ease away to the right. Cut off slightly left at this point, climbing gently up the field, to the right of a pool, and to cross another path at the boundary. Follow the tractor track ahead as it begins to climb left by Nitchells Coppice. At the next fence, the track curves through a gateway and continues up the hill to the top tapering corner.

16. Go through a gate at this point, climbing once more with the hedge to your right. Go through another gate, still climbing. At the summit, keep ahead through a stile by a large oak tree and to the left of a small wood. You now enter the Grey Valley, one of the most secluded parts of Herefordshire. Follow the hedge down the bank to another hedge and cross the stile. In the next field the way is slightly right towards the house at the road junction. Exit, by way of a stile, onto the road.

17. Turn left here and walk for a short distance until a stile appears on the right. Cross this and keep company with the hedge on your left until another stile is reached. Cross it and proceed ahead to cross a stream by way of a footbridge. Walk ahead along a hedge which leads to a stile, onto a green lane. Follow this to a road and bear left to climb up a steep hill into the isolated hamlet of Kerry's Gate. Just beyond the houses and telephone, turn right at the road junction to descend into the Dore valley by way of Blackbush farm.

18. Not far beyond the farm, at a sharp right hand bend, turn left to join a beautiful path to Abbeydore. The path leads into the housing of Riverdale (signposted). After the last house on the left, a path bears left behind a garage to a little gate leading into the field. Some walkers

simply continue through the allotments to cross a stile behind the old pig sty. Other locals simply continue ahead into the field at the gate by the signpost before Riverdale on a track, which leads into the field through a gap.

19. Whichever way you choose head for a stile in the next field boundary and once across bear very slightly right across the next field to a stile near to the banks of the River Dore. Cross this and keep ahead again through another rich meadow to another stile. Cross this and proceed ahead beneath the wooded bluff and by the river fording place. Go straight ahead along the riverside, through field boundaries at the gateways until the village of Abbeydore can be seen in the distance. Here, the gateway leads to a corralled section of path beneath a row of hazel trees to a small gate and to a stile exiting onto the road by Abbeydore Court.

20. Turn left to pass by the court and gardens but then turn right along a track after a concrete drive and before a stone built house. The lane soon brings the walker to the fence of a Ministry of Defence installation. Keep to the right by going through the kissing gate and follow the path as it curves right and then shortly left to a bridge over the river.

21. Head just to the left of the abbey, across the narrow enclosure to a sleeper bridge and kissing gate. Then go ahead to another kissing gate to the abbey churchyard surrounded by a farm and home orchard, a reflection of Herefordshire in times gone by. Walk up the path to the abbey entrance gate and the B4347.

ABBEYDORE TO ABERGAVENNY (Y FENNI)

START: Abbeydore church

DISTANCE: 27 km (17 ml)

MAPS: Pathfinder Sheets 1039 Golden Valley, 1063 Longtown and Pandy, and 1086 Abergavenny

ROUTE DESCRIPTION

This lengthy section can be divided into two by using a cut off point at The Old Pandy Inn. The route climbs over the windswept common of Ewyas Harold to the village of the same name, tucked between the Dulas Brook and River Dore. It then climbs to some of Herefordshire's wildest countryside between the hamlets of Rowlestone and Walterstone on the very borders of Wales. Marches Way then enters the Brecon Beacons National Park and along the banks of the Afon Honddu to Llanfihangel. It is then a matter of the challenge of Skirrid, a mountain of mystery before descending to Abergavenny along paths and back lanes.

FEATURES

Rowlestone

The hamlet of Rowlestone comprises a few farms and house nestled around the impressive church dating from the 12th century with a particularly fine carved south doorway.

Llancillo Chapel

This isolated chapel, with no road access, dates from early times but considerably restored throughout the ages. The stone gravestones dating from previous centuries provide an insight into local social history. Nearby is a castle mound not far from the ancient Llancillo court farmhouse.

Churches and paths

The early Christian church brought with it a thread of footpaths throughout the parish and many of these networks survive to this day. Schocklach and Llancillo are two good examples of very old path networks remaining. Many of the churches linked by Marches Way reflect the distinctive architecture of the Normans. There was at least one school of sculpture practising in the borderlands and their work can be seen most vividly in church doorways which still remain. Gargoyles and other embellishments also reflect the skills of these craftsmen. Kilpeck in Herefordshire (a few miles off Marches Way) is perhaps the best example of their work.

Walterstone

The old castle mound stands near to the church as does the inn, The Carpenters Arms. Marches Way also passes Walterstone Common and an old communal pump can be seen here. The route also passes near to Walterstone Camp, an Iron Age hillfort. Between the ramparts there is a secret garden planted in times past but now becoming overgrown and something of a curiosity.

Llanfihangel Crucorney

Llanfihangel stands at the entrance to the Vale of Ewyas, which leads to Llanthony Abbey and the Black Mountains. Its little church sits on a ridge overlooking the village which comprises a garage, inn and shop cum cafe, and scattered housing.

Llanfihangel court, a Tudor mansion where King Charles I (yes King Charles again) stayed during the English Civil War, is skirted by Marches Way and is open to the public on certain days in the summer.

The Skirrid Mountain

The Skirrid Mountain or Ysgyryd Fawr in Welsh was a place of worship in previous centuries, with a small chapel on the summit. The unusual shape of the hillside has led to several explanations about the huge split on the western slopes, including the work of the devil. Or could it possibly have been a local giant?

Abergavenny

Standing between the confluence of the Afon Gafenni and the Usk, Abergavenny (Y Fenni) was once a fortress town nestled between the surrounding mountains of the Blorenge, Sugar Loaf and The Skirrid. It is the starting point for many expeditions into the Brecon Beacons National Park and the lower Vale of Usk. The Museum at the Abergavenny castle houses a local collection including a Welsh kitchen and old saddler's shop. Those who fancy a walk around the town should buy the leaflet "A Walk Around Abergavenny", packed with information about local history.

Ewyas Harold Post Office, with the church peeping behind

REFRESHMENT

The Dog at Ewyas Harold is a lovely little pub open from 11.00 am until 2.30 pm Monday to Saturday and from 6.30 pm in the evenings, serving Wadsworths and Brains ales, and bar snacks. Usual Sunday hours prevail. Next door stands The Temple Bar.

The Carpenters Arms at Walterstone is a smashing old pub, open all day Monday to Saturday and usual hours on Sundays. It serves food and a pint of Wadworth's 6X straight from the barrel. Much of the inn is over 300 years old and the black leaded cooking range, original flagged floors and warm welcome make the place a joy to visit.

The Old Pandy Inn at Pandy is equally as friendly and serves a range of draught beers including Brains from Cardiff and Smiles from Bristol. There is also a restaurant, open Wednesday to Saturday evenings and Sunday lunchtime. One part of this area is set aside for families. The Old Pandy is open from 1130 until 3 pm weekdays, all day Saturdays and usual hours on Sunday.

The Lancaster Arms lies between Pandy and Llanfihangel and opens at noon every day, closing at about 2 pm in the winter and later in the summer. It re-opens at 7pm but earlier in the summer. The Lancaster serves two good brews from Wales, Brains SA and Felinfoel Cambrian on draught, offers meals and accommodation (0873) 890699, but is not really equipped for children.

The **Skirrid Mountain Inn** at Llanfihangel is open from 11.30 until 3 pm on Monday to Saturday (but this could be all day in the summer) and from 7 pm in the evenings. It serves Courage and John Smiths draught beers and food in very old surroundings. The inn dates back to 1110 and through the centuries has been an ale and court house. Many a rogue would have been sentenced – and some hanged on the premises! Nowadays, the pub is simply a purveyor of fine food and drink. There is also accommodation. Tel: (0873)890258.

ACCOMMODATION

Rowlestone, Walterstone, Pandy and Llanfihangel have accommodation available as does Abergavenny.

PUBLIC TRANSPORT

Red and White run between Abergavenny, Pandy and Pontrilas near to Ewyas Harold. Tel: (06333) 5118.

THE WALK

1. From the entrance to Abbeydore cross the road, and a stile on the other side of the road. Climb up the field very slightly right to cross a stile and continue ahead up to the next field boundary. Go left here and follow the hedge to a corner by a cottage where a stile by a gate leads onto Ewyas Harold Common. The description below will, hopefully, guide the walker across the Common. There are dozens of criss-crossing paths however, and tracks and several routes down off the common into Ewyas Harold village. Simply endeavour to keep along the ridge and bear slightly right, i.e. south east.

2. Walk a few paces ahead and bear left along a main green track, passing a bungalow on the left and shortly note a cottage on the left. Proceed ahead along the main track for a very short distance and at the next fork bear right along a lesser track which descends gently across the common to cross a track and several minor paths, as the common is well-walked by local people. The green path comes to another main fork. Bear left here to join a wider green track, usually with farm vehicles stored to the right near Prospect farm.

3. Walk a few paces ahead but turn right by an old working to drop down to a farm track. Go over this and walk down a green way to a stile, with a great view of Ewyas Harold village and the tree clad castle motte. This was once an important garrison. Cross the stile and walk down the field to cross another stile. Bear left to walk along a pavement by bungalows and go right into a playing field. Cut across to a gate and then walk ahead to a kissing gate into the churchyard. Follow the path through to exit by the post office and then turn left to pass The Dog public house and The Well shop.

4. From The Temple Bar public house, almost next door, take the road signposted to Rowlestone, over a bridge and by houses. This quiet back lane passes some houses, a small bridge and a pumping station on the right. Here, look for a barred gate just on the left. Follow the track up to another gate by a water trough and then make your way slightly right across this field, climbing towards the far corner by trees. There is a house to your right at the bottom of the field and a superb view back over Ewyas Harold.

5. Look for the stile hidden in the shade of the trees and cross this to join a sunken track. Bear right and walk a short distance up it to a lane. Go left for a few paces along the lane before crossing a stile on the right, set back from the road. Cross this and follow the field boundary on the right ahead, Graig farm being on the left. There are exquisite views down the Monnow valley and across southern Herefordshire from this vantage point.

6. Cross the stile in the field corner to enter a wood, but once again, the path soon exits into a large field. Head slightly left, parallel to the wood's edge on the left and cross the stile at the next boundary. In this next field, walk close to the field edge on the left as it curves gently left to a gap between two woods. Proceed directly ahead at first then after a hundred paces or so, head slightly right to aim for a gate to the right of an oak tree. Go through the gate and straight on to another gateway. In the next larger field head just to the left of a white cottage to cross a stile onto a road. Turn right and the lane leads down the hill and right to the hamlet of Rowlestone, a very quiet hamlet nestled around the church.

7. With Rowlestone church to your right and a telephone kiosk on the corner, go left through a barred gate. Proceed ahead down the field by the old barn and cider press to cross a stile and a small stream. Head downwards again, bearing slightly left now to pass through a gap beneath a hazel and hawthorn hedge. Continue into the valley to a ford over Cwm Brook and cross by way of a footbridge.

8. Climb the bank, heading diagonally left. As you approach the far hedge, look for a stile near a gateway. Cross the stile and the path bears slightly right across the field to meet a gully crossed by a bridge. In the next field head slightly right up to the top corner and cross a stile by two gates. Walk up the field following a line of oaks and look for a stile on the right over a thorn hedge. Once over, bear slightly left but keeping to the right of the small pool. The path leads down a bank laden with gorse and bracken, offering a good view of The Skirrid mountain ahead. The outline of Llancillo chapel lies in the trees below. The path drops alongside the wood to a stile by a barred gate. Cross the stile and bear slightly right towards the chapel and to the right of Llancillo court. The path leads down to a footbridge across a brook and passes to the right of a castle mound to the chapel.

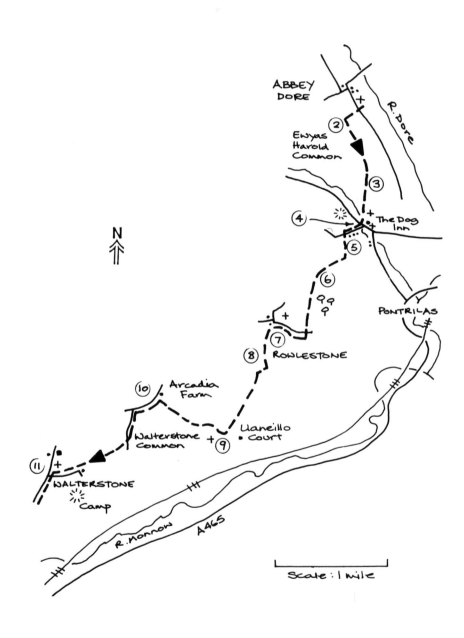

ABBEY DORE

R. Dore

Ewyas Harold Common

② ③

④ The Dog Inn

⑤

⑥

N

ROWLESTONE

⑧ ⑦

PONTRILAS

Arcadia Farm

⑩

Llaneillo Court

Walterstone Common ⑨

⑪ WALTERSTONE Camp

R. Monnow   A465

Scale : 1 mile

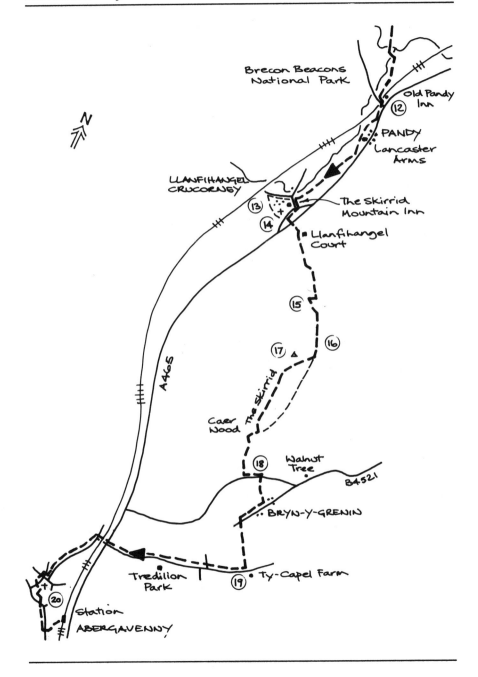

9. Go through the little gate into the churchyard. Pass to the left of the chapel and cross another stile into a narrow. orchard, and then over another stile. The path now bears slightly right to follow the field's edge with a stream below on the right. Cross a stile and keep straight on. Cross a stream at the next boundary and go ahead through a gateway. Keep ahead in the next field but bearing slightly left up the bank. Go through a gateway just to the right of an old barn, now keeping company with a hedge on the left. Proceed through another gateway and go ahead with Arcadia farm now in view. Cross a stile in the next hedge, go over the sleeper bridge and make your way diagonally across the field to exit through a gate onto a road by the farm.

10. Turn left and follow the road for a quarter of a mile into Walterstone Common. Pass by the common, complete with village pump and by a cottage, once an old chapel on the left. Look for a green lane on the right – it can become thick in growth during summer. The green lane gives out into a grassy area often encroached by bracken. Take a left turn here along a clearer path to another junction in a triangular wooded area. Bear right to meet two gates in succession. Go through both and head directly across the field to join a track through gaps in a hedge. Cross the stile and walk down the narrow and often wet track to another stile by the buildings of Grove farm. Bear right to join the main drive down to Rockyfold and onto a road. Go right, pass over the bridge and climb up the hill to a junction by Walterstone church and just beyond, the Carpenter's Arms.

11. Turn left at the junction and follow the road for nearly a mile to Allt-yr-Ynys, a hotel and restaurant to your left, and an old mill on the other side of the road. Ignore the road turning left, but soon after the hotel be vigilant for there is a stile in the hedge on the left and a footbridge to cross.

This section of path is walked by visitors staying in nearby Pandy and fishing folk, so is easy to follow. Go right and head across the field, away from the meander of the Monnow, to cross another stile. In the next field the path bears right along the field's edge near to the riverbank. This leads to another field where the path heads right again and onto a track. The footpath is shown on the map as passing through a gap after the sewerage works. It then follows a footpath alongside the track to a stile onto a road opposite a caravan site. Locals simply continue along the track to the road ahead. Turn left to pass under the railway and to the Old Pandy Inn.

12. Turn right to walk along a pavement adjacent to the busy A465 road to the bus stop (cut-off point for return to Hereford) and onwards to join the old road leading off to the right by cottages. Follow this to pass the Lancaster Arms, crossing the Offa's Dyke path. Re-join the main road, but only for a matter of metres before crossing a stile by a signpost to Pen-y-bont. Bear slightly left to cross a bridge and barred gate. There is a good view of a motte to the right from here, another early Marches fortress barely recognisable by now. Head very slightly right to cross a stile into a field usually full of caravans behind the Rising Sun restaurant. Go right to another stile and continue along the river bank to cross a stile into the next field where the walker exits onto a road. Turn left here for a short climb up to Llanfihangel, The Skirrid Mountain Inn and right for the church.

13. An alternative route is to turn right and at the junction bear left to pass by Bridge farm. As the walker approaches the railway line go left through a barred gate and walk ahead with a hedge to your left to go through another barred gate. Then, bear slightly left up the bank towards the Llanfihangel church, heading to the right of the church tower. A wooden stile leads into the churchyard and to the right of the church down steps to a gateway.

14. From Llanfihangel church, go ahead down a narrow tarmac lane to the main road. Cross with care and keep ahead towards Llanfihangel Court. The road bears right and begins to climb past this historic home and its charming farm outbuildings. The road becomes a rougher track and bears right to a gate just beyond a barn. The Skirrid stands a mile or so ahead, a challenge which few can resist. Even the Archdeacon Coxe made the climb in 1799 but according to the chronicles, he did feel a little giddy as a result. Head slightly left along a track to pass through two fields and gateways. The wire fence to the left curves left and at this point turn right. Head for a stile beneath a tree. Cross it and keep company with the hedge on the right up the bank to a stile by a gate and onto a road. Look back over the gate to Llanfihangel and this tree covered part of the Welsh Borderlands.

15. At the road, there is a white cottage to the left but your way is right for a pace or two, then left across a stile a metre or so up from the road by a newer gate. Walk up the field to pass to the left of an old barn and cross the stile. The area is often boggy and while it is tempting to follow the track, go through the gateway just to the right and across the field. Cross a stile in the next boundary by a gate and then beyond another small brook, bear right up the edge of the field to another stile. Cross this and now head slightly right, almost following the stream to the flanks of The Skirrid (Ysgyryd Fawr) itself. Towards the top corner of the field, there is a stile on the left. Avoid this, but continue up the field to a small gate leading onto National Trust land.

16. Proceed slightly left, by a National Trust waymarker stone, and then up the hillside slightly to the right, rather than up the steeper scrambles directly right. This path continues to climb at a civilised gradient to the top of the ridge, where you turn right towards the trig point and site of Saint Michael's chapel.

17. Retrace steps back along almost the entire length of the ridge, with views to Sugar Loaf (Y Fal) and Blorenge and over to England's undulating gently undulating pastures. The heavenly path now begins to descend steeply and it is necessary to keep slightly left along an eroded section to the fence below. Turn right here and continue to descend a little farther before going left over a stile. This path leads through Caer Wood, winding down to an information board and green lane to a car park on the main road.

18. Cross the road and turn left. Shortly before a house, cross a stile on the right. Walk up the field where the stile can be found just to the left of the top corner. Cross it and walk between fence and hedge to exit by cottages on a road through a quiet backwater known as Bryn-y-Gwenin. If in need of refreshment turn left for The Walnut Tree public house, just on the main B4521. Otherwise, turn right and follow the road to its end. There is a green lane ahead but your way is to the left, over a stile by a barred gate. Head slightly right across the field to cross another stile and then in the next field ahead to a junction of fences. Cross the stile here and go straight on again with a fence to your right. Cross yet another stile and now proceed slightly left over a larger field towards the farm buildings of Ty-capel farm. A stile by a gate exits onto a narrow tarmac·

lane. Bear right and follow this towards Abergavenny, a mile or so of road walking but with little traffic.

19. The lane shortly descends to a junction. Take the left fork and then go straight across to follow the narrow route into town passing first a golf course and then the entrance to Tredilion Park, with the ever watchful owls at the gateway. The road passes beneath the by-pass and railway (note the different styles of building) and to a main road. Go left and at the corner ahead down a quieter route, Ross Road. This leads virtually to the centre of town. At the main junction turn right into Lower Monk Street and then left into Monk Street to pass by the priory church. Go left down a narrow back lane by the Old Tythe Barn and, at the bottom, go through the car park, bus station (Swan Meadow) and Abergavenny Tourist Information Centre.

20. The route to Abergavenny railway station is straightforward. Turn left along the main road, Monmouth Road, where there is a variety of accommodation available, up to Station Road on the left. Walk up this road to pass The Great Western Hotel and to the station.

ABERGAVENNY TO PONYTPOOL

START: Abergavenny Railway station

DISTANCE: 23 kms (14 mls)

MAPS: Pathfinder Sheets 1086 Abergavenny and 1110 Pontypool

ROUTE DESCRIPTION

The path accompanies the River Usk to Llanfoist then rises to the Monouthshire and Brecon Canal, a tree-lined navigation offering haunting views of Sugar Loaf, Skirrid and across the Vale of Usk. Marches Way then climbs tracks and pathways to the idyllically situated Goose and Cuckoo public house in Upper Llanover, a fine place to be on a summer's day. There is a cut off route down to Llanover village but otherwise the path leads through forestry and lanes to the canal for the last stretch into Pontypool.

FEATURES

Llanfoist

The little church of Llanfoist dates from early times. It was extensively restored in the 1870s by a Mr Bailey in memory of his father, one of the great Iron masters in these parts.

The Monmouthshire and Brecon Canal

What an amazing survivor this navigation is. After disuse and neglect in the 1930s, the canal has been restored by the British Waterways Board with the assistance of the Brecon Beacons National Park into a thriving leisure route. Built originally as two separate canals -The Monmouthshire from Newport to north of Pontypool and The Brecknock and Abergavenny. The owners finally managed to link them up as the Monmouthshire and Brecon in 1812. There were several tramways from mines, kilns and works to the canal and the wharf and warehouse at Llanfoist would have been one such transhipment centre.

Llanover

The pretty estate village of Llanover owes its existence to a very dominant Lady Llanover, who lived at the hall in the last century. She was a popular benefactor in the neighbourhood and also much against the drinking of alcohol so had many of the local pubs closed. Twenty Welsh maidens accompanied her funeral cortege to Llanover church where she is buried.

Mamhilad

Legend has it that twenty monks carried a golden coffin bearing Saint Cadoc to this spot, where they were ambushed by marauding Danes. Try as they could the Danes could not lift the coffin nor chip any slithers of gold from it and the ground shuddered as they fled.

Pontypool

At Pontypool Park the Valley Inheritance museum is being developed and there are many local walks and trails. Pontypool town hall is a distinctive feature in the town centre, being Italianate in style. It was built by a local Iron master, Capel Hanbury Leigh, to celebrate the birth of his only son.

REFRESHMENT

The Goose and Cuckoo. A magnificent pub open from 11.30 until 3 pm and from 6.30 pm in the evening offering Brains and other draught beers. This CAMRA recommended pub serves food and offers a welcome break for walkers.

The Horseshoe Inn (also CAMRA recommended), at Mamhilad on the old drovers road has served weary travellers through the centuries. It offers Bass, Boddingtonas and Flowers original draught beers and serves food. The Horseshoe is open from 11.00 am until 3 pm and from 6 pm in the evening on Monday to Saturday and normal hours on Sundays. One past landlord was very keen on racing horses. When he took over the pub his horses began to lose. In desperation he re-hung the original horseshoe from the pub sign outside and his horses began to win again! The story is depicted in a picture at the bar.

The Goose and Cuckoo public house

ACCOMMODATION

Very limited. There is farmhouse accommodation adjacent to the Horseshoe inn and accommodation at Pontypool. Check at Tourist Information at Abergavenny.

PUBLIC TRANSPORT

Red and White run a service between Abergavenny and Pontypool on Monday to Saturday calling at Llanellen and Llanover. Contact them on (06333) 5118.

THE WALK

1. From Abergavenny railway station entrance bear left down Station Road passing by the Great Western Hotel on the right. At the main road turn right and pass by the Belmont public house. Not far beyond cross the road and go left down a lane between wall and hedge on the left by

(before) Mill Close. This leads to a path between hedges and onto a field. It then veers right over a footbridge near to the River Usk. There are exceptional views across the town to the Skirrid and Sugar Loaf from here.

Abergavenny and The Skirrid

2. Bear left towards the riverside by way of a smaller bridge and then turn right to follow the riverside path along to the Usk Bridge. Cross the road and turn left to go over the bridge. If not calling at The Bridge Inn on the other side, turn right to go under the old railway portals, attributed to the work of engineer John Gardner in 1868.

3. The road passes the cemetery, bears slightly left and descends beneath a main road to pass by a market garden and fields of vegetables. It climbs gently up to a road. Cross over and follow the road ahead by Llanfoist church, which soon becomes a wet and leafy lane. As it bears sharp left, continue ahead and then climb up steps to the canal, rather than continuing through the tunnel.

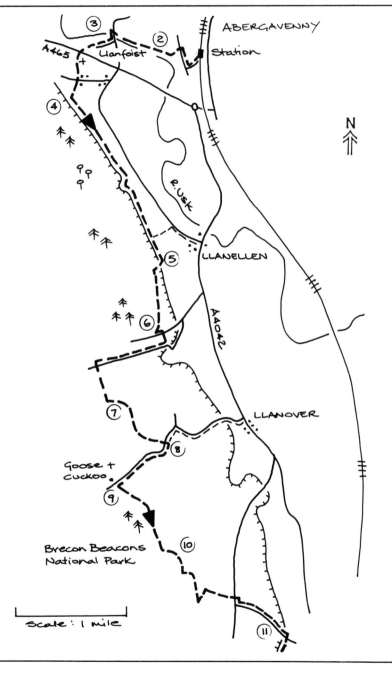

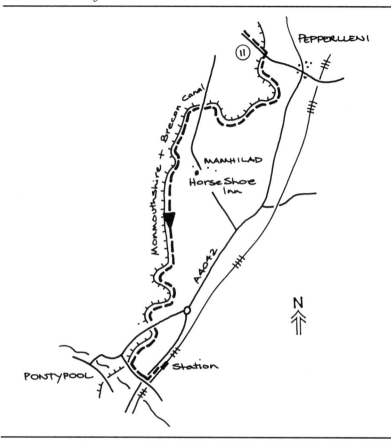

4. Turn left on the towpath, across from the old wharf and narrow boats on the opposite bank. The walking along this canal is very enjoyable given the elevation above surrounding countryside. Pass by Canal Cottage and then onto a splendid wooded section near Castell Prydydd, where the navigation curves dramatically into the hillside to cross a stream and on towards Llanellen. There is a stone stile on the left at Bridge number 92, just a short walk from the village, a possible cut-off point as buses run into Abergavenny and Pontypool from here.

5. At the next footbridge, the way leaves the canal to climb into the foothills of the Brecon Beacons National Park to the Goose and Cuckoo public house. Go over the footbridge and bear slightly left as signposted to the left of a barn. Cross a stile and join a wider track along the

woodland's edge. Turn left and follow this along the back of houses which leads ahead to a wider track and down to a road.

6. There is a telephone kiosk on the right at this point but turn left for a short section. As the road descends, cross a stile on the right into a field and follow the hedge on the right to cross another stile. Proceed ahead to cross a stile onto a road. Turn right and follow the road as it drops steeply and then climbs to a crossroads. Keep ahead, climbing remorselessly up the valley for about half a mile and at the next junction bear left along a narrow lane. Very soon, go right up a green track which rises up the valley sides, above two farmsteads below, and offering spectacular views across Gwent. At the next main junction turn left. A track curves right above Upper Llwyn-celyn farm to reach a road by a group of tall beech trees.

7. Almost opposite is a stile by a gate. Cross this and follow the green lane ahead alongside a row of fine trees as it curves left and through a gate to a group of tall trees. Walk ahead through the trees but, before the next field, the path cuts off right to a barn before bearing slightly left across the field to the far left corner. Many walkers simply keep to the left hand wall heading the direction of the left corner. Go over low level metal fencing to enter another piece of woodland. A few paces ahead bear slightly right to walk through the wood, keeping to the left of old workings and moving closer to fencing on the left as the path descends to a track. Go left and follow this to a road.

8. Those seeking to a cut off point at Llanover should bear left and at the next junction turn right by Caeffynon. Follow this narrow lane down to Llanover village passing over the canal at Bridge Number 81 and offering a link back to Marches Way. Those, however, seeking higher ground should bear right to follow the road as it climbs to The Goose and Cuckoo public house.

9. Retrace a few steps down from The Goose and Cuckoo and bear right as signposted into woodland. The path continues ahead until it reaches a junction above a house and descends left to a triangular junction of main tracks. Go right here and follow this to reach a main forestry track. Cross it and within a few paces, go up a lesser track on the right near the field boundary. Soon bear left again and at the next junction. This soon joins a main forestry access track again where you go right to cross it to re join

a green lane on the other side. At the next junction do not go left nor right. Keep ahead down a narrow path. As it descends bear left, ignoring a stile on the right and at the bottom turn left into a road.

10. This soon joins a more prominent access road leading to a junction. Turn right and then left at the next junction then right at the next one but only to turn next left again along the road to Penperlleni. This comes to a staggered crossroads, where you bear right and then left. Pass by a few houses and then soon the walker comes to a bridge over the canal once again. Those seeking a cut off point can continue along the road to The Goytre Inn at Penperlleni.

11. Go left onto the towpath and left again under the bridge and follow its winding course for several miles into Pontypool. There are opportunities to cut off at Mamhilad, by the unusual high level bridge to The Horseshoe Inn in the village. In Pontypool the path curves under a lower level modern bridge and then runs into a cutting with houses on the opposite bank. Before the next road bridge, a path climbs up to the left. Bear left for the short walk to the station road entrance on the left and down to Pontypool railway station, referred to more accurately in the heyday of steam as Pontypool Road.

PONTYPOOL TO NEWPORT

START: Pontypool Railway Station

DISTANCE: 20 kms (13 mls)

MAPS: Pathfinder Sheets 1110 Pontypool, 1130 Cwmbran and 1149 Newport.

ROUTE DESCRIPTION

The route leaves Pontypool across fields and along an old track to Llandegfedd reservoir and the beautiful Sôr valley. It climbs up to the village of Llanhennock then descends to Caerleon and across the tidal River Usk. Another climb through parkland brings the walker to the suburbs of Newport with views over the Severn Estuary.

FEATURES

Llandegfedd

The reservoir was completed in 1964, and supplies water to Cardiff and parts of Gwent. There is a yarn from these parts about a Llandegfedd reaper who, on his way home one night, was asked by a ghostly character to dismantle the stone of an old barn. There he would find gold, which he should then deposit in a local pool for safe keeping. Needless to say, the gold was never found and the reaper died. Two mile on is Llandegfedd village, described by a well-known local writer, Fred Hando, earlier in the century, as "That quaintest of all toy villages". It remains a charming place to visit.

Llanhennock

Settled around an old highway the village of Llanhennock has several unusual houses, including the Old Mackworth Arms and the local school. The church stands proudly against the windswept hillside with its distinctive tower a landmark seen from southern slopes.

Caerleon

The Romans built their garrison near to the banks of the Usk and the remains of the fortress and surrounding dwellings have been mapped out in Caerleon. The amphitheatre is by far the best preserved in the UK and has connections with the Arthurian legend. Even Tennyson came to gain inspiration from the site when writing about Arthur and the Round Table. Despite the traffic the little town of Caerleon is pleasant to stroll around and there is a museum near to the church.

Newport

Rich in industrial architecture and history, Newport is characterised by its unusual transporter bridge, built in the latter part of the last century with a lift 170 feet above the river and 650 feet in length. Newport used to be a very busy port and the Usk thronged with vessels and the small wharfs along Town Reach remain, although very little traffic now comes up the river. Newport castle stands defiantly by Newport Bridge (which has seen a few shipping and car collisions in its time) but is now dominated by the modern traffic system. Near to Newport is Tredegar House, a classic example of a King Charles II mansion and surrounded by extensive gardens.

REFRESHMENT

The Farmers Arms, Llandegfedd is open for refreshment. **The Wheatsheaf**, a Good Beer Guide entry, at Llanhennock, is open from noon until 3.30p.m., then from 5.30 p.m. on Mondays to Fridays. There is all-day opening on Saturdays and usual Sunday hours. The Wheatsheaf is a friendly old pub which serves draught Bass, Brains and Worthington Best as well as food.

ACCOMMODATION

There is accommodation at Caerleon and Newport.

PUBLIC TRANSPORT

There are very regular buses between Caerleon and Newport weekdays and also on Sundays. The villages in the Sôr valley have little or no public transport so there is no easy cut off until Caerleon.

Welsh Borderlands near Pontypool

THE WALK

1. Leave Pontypool railway station entrance by turning left along a railway road. This soon becomes a track, passing through a gateway on the right and along a rough track ahead, with bungalows to the right. Pass through a gateway into a field with woodland to the right and a farm ahead. Go through another gateway and as the track begins to curve left go right over a stile. Walk through this small field and cross a stile by a gate. Head very slightly left to cross a stile in the next field boundary. Bear slightly left and cross a stile at the edge of the wood, with a fine view back across to Pontypool. Continue ahead up the field with houses to the right, hopefully the extent of residential territory here for a while.

2. The path leads to a road. Turn left but only for a matter of one hundred paces or so. Bear right through a stile by a gate and head slightly left across the field, with views of Llandegfedd coming into sight on the right. This leads to a stile by a gate and onto a road. Turn right and right again at the next junction. Pass by farms and buildings, including an old pumphouse. The track becomes rougher and narrows just around the corner, soon becoming almost covered by a canopy of bushes. The track widens again and drops to the waters edge of an inlet where just beyond is a permissive path cutting left alongside the reservoir which some might wish to walk.

3. Otherwise, continue along the track up to and by Sluvad farm. Bear left on the road and prepare for a climb passing the water treatment plant. The road curves right by a cottage (where the permissive route re joins) and begins to descend to the reservoir. Look for a path leading off to the right through woodland, signposted to the Sôr Brook picnic site.

This is a lovely path, but a little tricky in places as it clings to the hillside when dipping and climbing through Cwm-bwrwch wood. The path levels and then leaves the wood to drop slightly and then climb through bracken before the final descent to the picnic site. There is a minor variation here. Follow the road down to the reservoir and as it bears left across the dam keep ahead and bear right along a path, with a helpful rail for the first section, which climbs up to join the path mentioned above. Bear left at the junction and onward to the picnic site.

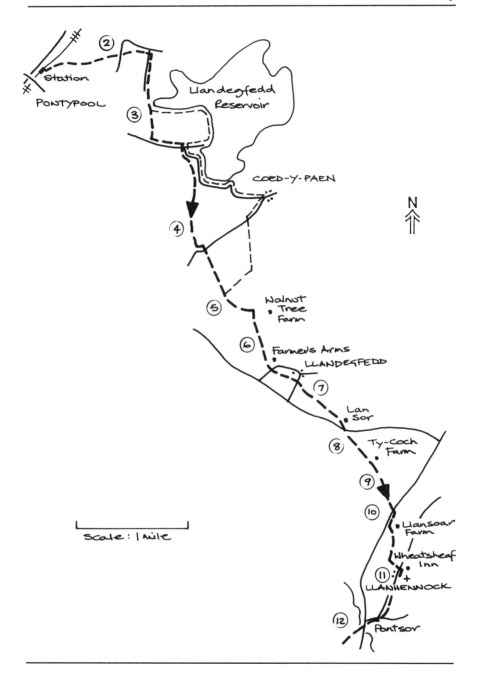

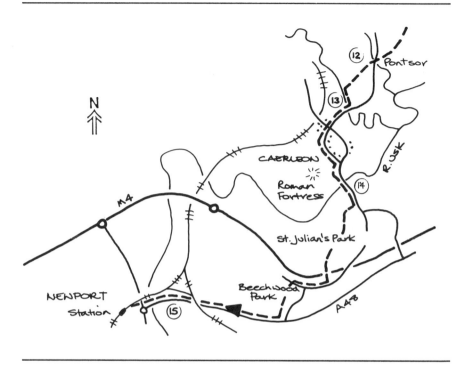

4. Leave the site by the main gate, and walk to the junction, turn left onto the road to Coed-y-Paen which curves sharply right over the Sôr brook and begins to rise. Within a hundred paces look for a path on the right signposted to Llandegfedd village through a gate in a state of collapse (it might be renewed!). The well-worn path leads off slightly right into a wood by the brook, keeping to the top of the bank. Go through a gateway and keep ahead, cutting off the meanders, to a narrower stretch between wood and brook where a stile is crossed. Continue ahead through a short field to cross another stile. Go straight ahead across the next field to cross a footbridge and then left to go through a gate and at the track go right.

5. Join an access road and bear left along it to walk beneath a wooded slope soon to cross the Sôr Brook again with the ancient Walnut Tree farm viewed on the hillside ahead. Once over the bridge and, before the next gateway, go right over a stile on the right and into a pasture. Then, turn left to head towards a footbridge across a tributary brook. Cross the bridge and keep to the corner on a level path. Head very slightly right

for a stile mid way along a hedge opposite and then proceed ahead once again in a similar direction to a footbridge leading into a wood.

6. Cross the footbridge and bear left. The path meets another coming in from the left and continues ahead along the bottom of a bracken laden bank. Cross a stile and into a wood again to climb up to another stile and then descend to the village of Llandegfedd. Go left and on the left is The Farmers Arms. Opposite it is a path passing through a narrow passage to a field. Then along a well worn path to cross a stile by a gate and ahead to cross another stile leading onto a road.

7. Go slightly left over the road and then right into a field as signposted to Lan Sôr. Walk ahead by the brook at first then cut across a meander bearing slightly left to a footbridge. On the other bank turn right to go over a stile in the next hedge. Keep ahead but begin to move closer to the brook on the right and cross another stile into the next field where the walker bears slightly left to exit by way of a stile near a gate. Go left on the road to pass by Lan Sôr and walk to a corner where a stile leads into a field on ghe right. The path bears slightly left across the field to cross a track by way of gates.

8. Walk straight on through fields, passing through two gates towards Ty-Coch farm. Head towards a barn and pass through a gate to the right of it. Walk up the track on the right to meet another track and bear right to descend to a corner where there is a stile on the left in a very thick hedge.

9. Head slightly left across a field moving closer to the brook and then head across a meander in the direction of Llansoar Fawr farm on the hillside. Cross a footbridge over a drainage ditch and walk straight on to a stile adjacent to a gate leading to a main road.

10. Go right and soon cross the road and walk up the drive towards Llansoar Fawr farm. By large barns, look for a gate on the right, near a bungalow on the left, to a green track climbing the hillside to a fork. Your way, however, is to climb up to a stile in the middle beneath trees. Cross the stile and keep company with a hedge on the right. Shortly, head slightly left, after trees, up the hillside to a gate. There are farms below. Go through the gate and bear slightly left across a large field to pass to the right of an electric telegraph pole and heading towards the

left of a red roofed house in the village of Llanhennock. The path exits by way of a gate onto a road at the top right field corner.

11. The Wheatsheaf public house stands on the left, the old Mackworth Arms and a telephone kiosk almost in front and Llanhennock church just to the right. Turn right on the road which leads down to the main road at Pont Sôr. Cross it and go left for a short section before turning right along a dirt track which soon bears right. Your way is ahead along a wire fenced track.

The church, Llanhennock

12. Just beyond the end of the garden as the track curves right into a sunken lane go left through a gate and head slightly left up the field towards three electric telegraph poles. Cross a stile and head very slightly right over rough ground and still climbing. Cross a stile in a fence and then head slightly left towards a stile not easily seen at first. This spot offers a grand view of Caerleon as the path leads slightly left down the hillside with an old farm to the right across the field. The path begins to curve left towards the bottom left corner of the field where a stile leads onto a lane between houses.

13. Turn left and very shortly leave the lane to keep near the Afon Lwyd, along a short path overgrown with stinking hellibore and other water loving plants. The paths leads to a road where the walker bears right to cross a bridge and a short walk along Usk Road into Caerleon. At the crossroads continue ahead and follow Goldcroft around to the town centre (High Street) where there are inns, restaurants and shops. Turn next right along White Hart lane by the White Hart public house leading to the main road near the River Usk. Cross the road and walk over the bridge. Pass by the Ship Inn and keeping to the left fork, known as New Road (B4236) rather then the main B4596 road.

14. The road rises up to cottages and opposite a road turning, Bulmore Road, on the left, bear first right along a track by Ashwell Cottages into a green lane, then through a gate and into a field. Keep ahead to go through a kissing gate into Saint Julian's Park. Go left and climb up through woodland to a parting of paths. Keep to the path bearing gently right and keep climbing to parkland to the right of Christchurch cemetery. There are excellent views of the Usk and Newport from this leafier suburb. A path leads to a concrete bridge across the motorway and curves around into Christchurch Road. Go right and shortly turn left down Beechwood road. Alternatively, theres a gate leading into Beechwood Park which is more attractive. At the bottom join the busy Chepstow Road. Turn right to walk a mile into town or simply catch one of the very frequent buses to avoid a mile of none-too-pleasant walking.

15. The path crosses the River Usk above Town Reach and passes under an underpass signposted to Newport railway station. Continue ahead to the top of Cambrian Road where an underpass on the right brings the walker to the station entrance.

NEWPORT TO TONGWYNLAIS

START: Newport Railway Station

DISTANCE: 24 kms (15 mls)

MAPS: Pathfinder Sheets 1149 Newport and 1148 Ponty-pridd (South) and Caerphilly.

ROUTE DESCRIPTION

Leaving Newport over Allt-yr-yn and the Monmouthshire and Brecon canal, the route rises to the Fourteen Locks Visitor centre and across the valley of the Afon Ebbw to Rhiwderin and wilder parts. Marches Way continues through woodland and field paths to Draethen to join the Rhymney Valley Ridgeway path to Rudry. From here, the ridgeway path offers magnificent views up the valleys and to Cardiff and the estuary. It descends through woodlands to Tongwynlais.

FEATURES

Fourteen Locks

The Crumlin branch of the Monmouth and Brecon canal is fascinating. Only partly filled with water and rich in wildlife, this once busy artery is now quiet – except for the roar of the motorway. The Visitor Centre explains the development of the canal.

Draethen

A quiet village nestled around a tributary stream feeding into the Afon Ebbw. The valley leading up to Rudry would have supported several small mills at one time. Draethen has a nursery which specialises in herbs and grape vines for those who enjoy a kitchen garden.

Nearby, Marches Way passes the ancient homestead, Ruperra Castle, which is unfortunately not open to the public.

Rudry

The old church of Rudry can be seen through the trees on Marches Way as can Caerphilly town and castle a little farther along. This Ridgeway section offers magnificent views for miles around and is a particular joy on a fine summers eve.

Castell Coch

Described as a fairy tale castle, this architectural gem from the last century was designed by William Burgess for the third Marquess of Bute. It is open to the public.

REFRESHMENT

Marches Way passes a few pubs in the Rogerstone area, including **The Rising Sun** which is open from 11.00 am until 3 pm and then from 5.30 pm onwards on Monday to Saturday (Normal Sunday hours), offering Courage and John Smiths draught beers and food. **The Tredegar Arms**, a Good Beer Guide entry, opens from 11.30 am until 3 pm and from 6pm in the evenings (Normal Sunday hours) serves Brains Dark, Courage beers and often a guest beer too. It also serves food.

There are other watering holes en route including the Rhiwderin Inn at Rhiwderin (CAMRA Listed), the Hollybush Inn (also CAMRA listed) at Draethen and the Maenllwyd Arms at Rudry. There are also public houses in Tongwynlais, and all are open at lunchtime and evening. The walker need not go thirsty on a hot summer's day.

ACCOMMODATION

Limited accommodation in the Tongwynlais area.

PUBLIC TRANSPORT

There is a regular bus service from Newport to Rogerstone, Rhiwderin and Little Machen for Draethen allowing cut-off points or a ride out of Newport to shorten the walk along the ridgeway. Contact Gwent County Council for details on (0633) 838838.

Newport Transporter Bridge during construction, 1905 (Newport Museum and Art Gallery)

THE WALK

1. From Newport railway station entrance walk through the underpass signposted to Devon Place. Turn left to walk along this road and then righf into Godfrey road by the Civic Centre. Proceed to the top of the street, walk a few steps right and then turn immediately left into Allt-yr-yn Avenue, passing by Saint Mark's Crescent. Continue ahead along Allt-yr-yn Avenue into Allt-yr-yn Road. This climbs up through a residential quarter to the brow. Just beyond, turn right and after Allt-Yr-Yn Lodge turn second left down a track.

2. The views are good and the hillside has been chosen as a nature park by the Newport Borough and Gwent Wildlife Group. Pity about the roar of the motorway below. The track passes near to the delightfully named Strawberry farm and then to a bridge over the Monmouthshire and Brecon canal. Turn left and follow the towpath for about a mile before it

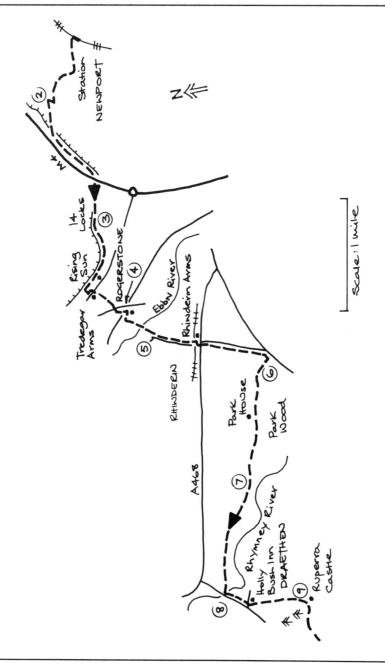

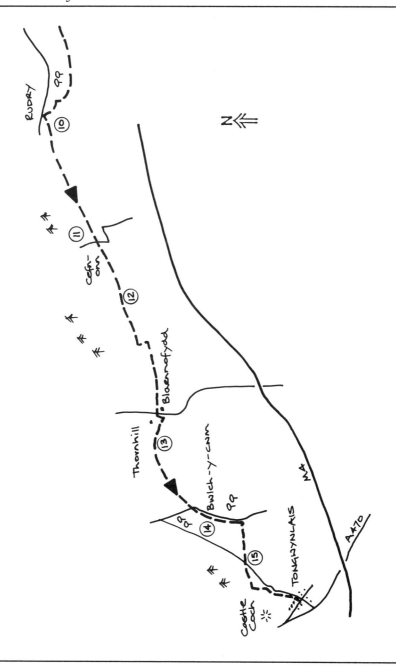

joins the Sirhowy Walk and plunges beneath the motorway as a concrete underpass, temporarily devoid of canal.

The path then climbs lock sides of Fourteen Locks, passes a farm and continues by locks to a pool by the Visitor Centre. Notice the old Great Western diamond railway signs.

3. Continue ahead along the towpath, as the canal borders a road and The Rising Sun public house. Cross a bridge, with a roundabout to your left, but continue to the next bridge where the walker bears left as signposted down a narrow lane to the main Cefn road. Cross the road and turn left for the short walk to the Tredegar Arms. Turn right to walk down Bethesda Place and then bear next left. This leads to a series of bollards where the path heads slightly left between a fence and houses. This exits onto another road, Saint John's Crescent, by The Old Globe public house. Cross the road and turn left to go over the bridge. Then, turn right to pass by the shop as signposted to Rhiwderin.

4. The road leads to a sports ground, where you bear left to pass between the hall, cricket pitch and tennis courts. It then passes between high fences to a bridge over the Afon Ebbw. Proceed up through the wood to an iron gate and then bear right to walk ahead, keeping company with the hedge on the left. It exits onto a very quiet lane by way of a kissing gate.

5. Turn left to walk along the narrow road into Rhiwderin. Keep ahead to cross the railway and come to a main road. Go left for the Rhiwderin Inn but your way is to cross the road, turn right and then next left up a steep minor road. Pass Brynhedydd and continue to a main road junction opposite the entrance to the Farmers Daughter restaurant. Bear right and turn next right on a lane to Cwrt-y-llaca and Parkwood House. Pass by a house and farther down the lane, as another house is approached, bear left to go through a barred gate and into Park Wood.

6. The path proceeds ahead near to the hedge on the right with streams crossing the path in places so it can become very wet. The path begins to curve left moving deeper into the wood and comes to a fork. Keep right here and fields can still be seen on the right through the trees.

The path, much wider now, begins to climb a little and there is a wicket gate on the right. Do not go through it but continue ahead to join a track coming into the wood from a barn. Bear slightly left here and continue until another gateway leading into fields. Just before this cut right through the woodland along a narrower path once again. This comes to a junction. Bear left and follow this track until it comes to a stile by a gate into a field.

7. Turn right and cross a stile and then go left to cross sheep pen fencing and then bear right to proceed along a hedge on the right. Keep ahead through two gateways and along a farm track with Plas Machen to the right. The track shortly bears left by drainage channels and ahead to a gateway. Once through keep ahead to another gateway with a group of trees just to the left of it. Go through it and then bear diagonally left across a field to cross a small sleeper bridge across a drainage channel and then go over a stile. Walk ahead in the next field to a stile situated just to the right of a bridge spanning the Afon Rhymney.

8. Go left to cross the bridge and walk up the road into Draethen village. The road passes by houses and the Hollybush Inn stands just to the left across a small bridge. The walker passes alongside the pub to cross a stile and bear slightly right up the field to another stile into woodland. Continue to climb up the well worn path to a main junction. Go right here but within a matter of 200 metres go left at the next fork, still climbing for a while. Cross another track and drop down onto a track by the walled gardens of Ruperra Castle.

9. Turn right and walk up the drive, to pass to the left of the White House and along a slight ridge offering views across the Severn Estuary to the West Country. This eventually gives out by houses onto a minor road. Turn right and follow the road as it dips and then climbs steeply to Rudry.

10. Turn left at the junction and opposite the Maenllwyd Inn go left up steps, passing by picnic tables belonging to the pub to a stile. Cross this and a track, following a yellow arrow waymark. Keep ahead on a main forest track, towards an electricity pylon and avoiding turns to the left. The track continues to gain ground along the ridge to meet an iron gate. Go through it and walk ahead to a stile. This leads into an older deciduous wood, the path winding slightly left and then right. Soon you

reach an upland pasture segregated by a barbed wire fence. The path leads down a bank to pass on the left the outbuildings of Plas farm at Cefn Onn, which is a blessing – for the cattle make it very messy in winter.

11. Go over the road and continue ahead along a ridge track. The views up the valleys are superb and later those to the east, across the Severn Estuary are equally good. The track comes to a small and large gate. Go through the former and at the next junction bear right down the hillside and very shortly turn left along a narrower and greener track (as signposted by a blue waymark) rather than descending the main track. This skirts a quarry and leads into woodland. The path curves to the left to a small gate by a barred one. Go through it and continue down the bank for a hundred paces or so. Your way is to the right to enter woodland again through a gate.

12. Go through a heavy barred gate and ahead again through gateposts and onwards. This is waymarked with blue arrows through to a point before Blaen Nofydd farm, where the track forks right to the main A469 road at Thornhill. Cross the road and turn left but then go next right along a track. Keep ahead at the junction through a farm yard and through barred gates to the left of farm buildings to a gateway ahead.

13. Proceed to the next gateway where you bear slightly left across the field, rather than right as waymarked on the Ridgeway Path which you now leave. Your path crosses a trickle of a stream and then begins to curve slightly right to a much wider brook, Nant Cwmnofydd, cascading down a dip hidden by tree cover. The track continues ahead through another pasture to pass by old farm buildings and in a short distance by houses at Bwlch-y-Cwm.

14. Turn left along the road down Rhiwbina Hill and at the edge of the wood, with houses to the left, go right over stile leading into the woodland. Follow the bridleway at first but then choose the path ahead leading down the hill, with the boundary to your left. The path is often encroached by brambles and is quite steep in places. It eventually joins another main path coming in from the right in the valley bottom of Nant-y-Fforest. Turn left and follow the path across a bridge over the stream to a road.

15. Go over the road to join a track leading up to the Visitor Centre, where there is an information board and picnic tables. The path however, climbs slightly right at this point to meet another path. Go left down the hill and meet the road once again. Turn right here and follow the road to a crossroads in Tongwynlais, where there are shops. The Lewis Arms and Cardiff Castle public houses stand on opposite sides of the road.

Castell Coch (Wales Tourist Board)

TONGWYNLAIS TO CARDIFF

START: The Crossroads at Tongwynlais

DISTANCE: 11 kms (7 mls)

MAPS: Pathfinder sheets 1148 Pontypridd (South) and Caerphilly, and 1165 Cardiff and Penarth.

ROUTE DESCRIPTION

A walk which joins several paths and the Three Castles cycle route into Cardiff by way of the Taff Vale. The walk hugs the riverbank for the most part. Considering the industrial and highway encroachment, it is very pleasant, particularly towards Cardiff city where the gardens are superb.

FEATURES

Llandaff

The modern cathedral stands in tranquil gardens near to the Taff. There have been several places of worship on the site since Celtic times. The last cathedral was destroyed during the Second World War and the modern building seen today is much admired by the local community. A short detour across the river can easily be made.

Cardiff

It might well be small as capital cities go but it is full of energy and interest. Home to the World Harp festival and other cultural events Cardiff excels in bringing events to Wales, not to mention the sporting fraternity to Cardiff Arms Park for rugby internationals, an experience in its own right. Cardiff Castle and the National Museum are excellent as is the Welsh Folk Museum at nearby Saint Fagan's. The docklands are being developed for leisure purposes and Cardiff is destined to become one of Europe's major waterfront cities.

REFRESHMENT

There are restaurants, cafes and inns galore in Cardiff.

ACCOMMODATION

Plentiful supply in and around Cardiff.

PUBLIC TRANSPORT

From Tongwynlais, it is possible to return to Cardiff by bus or walk to Radyr station (just over a mile on Marches Way) to catch one of the "Valleys" trains into Cardiff.

THE WALK

The walk follows, for the most part, a well recognised Taff Valley Heritage trail, part of the Taff Valley cycle route and is therefore very easy to follow, with several waymarks to guide the walker.

1. Cross the main road in Tongwynlais by the Lewis Arms and Cardiff Castle public houses to proceed down Market Street. Pass by the chapel and then go through an appalling subway to a more tranquil quarter of Ivy House farm. The path leads through a kissing gate and by the fast flowing waters of the Afon Taff.

2. This riverside path beneath the bows of oak and sycamore, ash and lime soon crosses a track and joins the cycleway. This passes underneath a vast concrete arch and then your way is through the gap stile on the right to join another stretch of easy walking through lush growth near to the river bank. Within half a mile there is a bridge on the right leading to Radyr railway station, a useful cut-off point for weary walkers.

3. The route, however, proceeds ahead, diverting along a slightly higher level path for a short distance. It then drops by playing fields on the left and a newer housing estate to the right where factories once stood. The road joins another after a small works. Turn right and walk along this residential road for about a quarter of a mile along Ty Mawr road. Once under the railway bridge join the path on the right into Hailey Park.

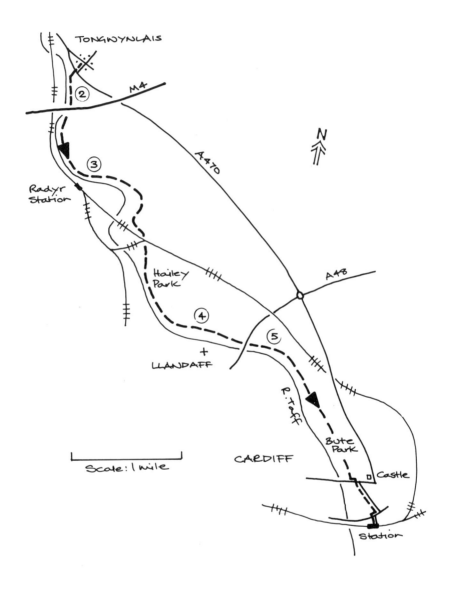

4. Pass by the rugby club and grounds, with Llandaff cathedral ahead in the near distance. Your way is ahead to pass by tennis courts and to a road. Keep ahead along the river to the next road and bridge, but go through the short underpass. The way is ahead, keeping to paths and tracks near to the Taff, often shared with many more cyclists now.

5. The main path moves away from the river but wherever possible keep to the riverside paths in Bute Park, a major attraction in Cardiff city. The gardens become more formal and those wishing to visit the castle should seek paths to the left. Otherwise, the riverside path exits on to Castle Street by a bridge. Turn left, cross to bear right into Heol-y-Porth (Westgate Street) with Cardiff Arms Park on your right. This soon joins Wood Street where your way is right and then left by the bus station and to Cardiff Central Station.

Cardiff Castle, from Bute Park (Wales Tourist Board)

Footnote . . .

It is a time of reflection. Perhaps, sitting at a quayside bar down the old docks or at Cardiff Central waiting for the homeward train, the walker might well cast a thought back to the trials and tribulations of Marches Way but more so to the joys of this long distance path.

It could only have been a few hours ago that you stood on the Ridgeway above Caerphilly and looked out across the expanse of Cardiff to the Severn estuary, to the tops of the valleys and the Brecon Beacons beyond. Only a day or two ago when you descended to Llancillo church – one of the most peaceful places on earth – or climbed with vigour the challenging Skirrid.

However far you have walked along the route, the author hopes that you feel a sense of satisfaction of being on Marches Way, a satisfaction of really getting to know at first hand this charming borderland country. For this understanding can only be achieved when travelling by foot. Raise a glass of cheer to your endeavours and whisper the words of Housman: "The quietest place under the sun". Let us hope the Marches remains so.